Some GAVE ALL

FOUR STORIES OF MISSIONARY MARTYRS

ELLEN CAUGHEY

BARBOUR
PUBLISHING

© 2002 by Barbour Publishing, Inc.

ISBN 1-59789-119-3

All rights reserved. No part of this publication may be reproduced or transmitted in any form or by any means without written permission of the publisher.

Churches and other non-commercial interests may reproduce portions of this book without the express written permission of Barbour Publishing, provided that the text does not exceed 500 words or 5 percent of the entire book, whichever is less, and that the text is not material quoted from another publisher. When reproducing text from this book, include the following credit line: "From *Some Gave All,* published by Barbour Publishing, Inc. Used by permission."

All scripture quotations are taken from the King James Version of the Bible.

Cover illustration © Dick Bobnick
Cover design by Douglas Miller (mhpubarts.com)

Published by Barbour Publishing, Inc., P.O. Box 719, Uhrichsville, OH 44683, www.barbourbooks.com

Our mission is to publish and distribute inspirational products offering exceptional value and biblical encouragement to the masses.

Member of the
Evangelical Christian
Publishers Association

Printed in the United States of America.
5 4 3 2 1

INTRODUCTION

The four Christian missionaries described in this book will not all be defined by the most traditional definition of martyr. Only one, Nate Saint, died as a direct result of his Christian witness. But the other three—John Birch, Betty Olsen, and Lottie Moon—should still, without doubt, be considered under the same heading. Indeed, they died because they had given all they had to spread the gospel to the ends of the earth.

Two were the children of missionaries, two served in the military, three never married, and three were college graduates, but there are few other similarities among the four. What they really shared, what was most important to each of them in the final years of their lives, was a burning desire from the core of their beings to tell others about Jesus.

Missionaries, and especially missionary martyrs, are often held up to the rest of us as extraordinary examples of overwhelming devotion to the Christian cause. But as you will read in the pages that follow, the missionaries' commitment may have been extraordinary, but the individuals were completely ordinary. Like the rest of us, they had human needs and desires. They had dreams that had to be forgotten or discarded. They were known, at times, to flounder, having lost their hope.

But they kept going, kept trusting, and kept praying. And then, because of where they were, who they were, and whom they were serving, they were called to make the ultimate sacrifice.

JOHN BIRCH

ONE

Shangrao, China—April 1942

Ever since Pearl Harbor, money had been a problem. Now in the last three days the situation had become almost impossible for Baptist missionary John Birch. Even though Shangrao was still in "Free China," that is, free from Japanese occupation, no bank in Kiangsi Province would cash American traveler's checks anymore.

Alone in his cottage, John sat down on a simple wooden chair to think. He had radioed, cabled, and sent missives via airmail to his missionary headquarters in Chicago and received no answer. Communication in the best of times was difficult, he had to admit. With the world at war, he had little reason to expect a reply. To complicate matters, for the past several months he had had company. Another missionary, a native Chinese Christian, had risked his life to come all the way from Japanese-occupied Shanghai to Shangrao. Perhaps there, he reasoned, John would be able to receive funds that were meant for the Shanghai base as well. Whatever reserves the missionaries there had were fast running out.

Unknown to his Shanghai guest, for the last three days John had been completely destitute. It was now April 16, and the money was gone. In the current state of affairs, the traveler's checks he had saved from his fifty-dollar-a-month salary were worthless.

Yet, despite the dire scenario, John's faith was unshakable. He had grown up poor, gone to school poor, and graduated from seminary with few possessions, except for a one-way ticket aboard a freighter from Seattle to China. God had brought him to this province in southeastern China to bring spiritual and physical help to a distraught people. Would He force him to abandon this mission when the specter of war was looming closer with every day?

John's reverie was suddenly interrupted by excited voices outside, the dissonant Chinese syllables portending important news. Jumping up from his chair, the wiry American raced down the dusty street toward the small crowd that had gathered. His "native brother" from Shanghai was in the middle of the group, gesticulating wildly.

"John, there's news from Chinese army headquarters in Hangchow," he said, pointing to the town official's office. "They're willing to cash traveler's checks from American banks—at last! And they can cable the money to us here. Perhaps I can return to Shanghai tomorrow?"

Elated and relieved, John grasped the shoulders of his fellow missionary and then shook hands with the other native Christians who were as desperate as he for supplies. "That's good news, my friend," John finally said. "But you're wrong about one thing. *You're* not going to Shanghai tomorrow. We'll go together, at least for a ways. With all that change in your pocket, you're too important to lose," he said, breaking into his familiar grin, followed by his familiar laugh. All around him the worried grooves of the weathered, sunburned faces seemed to soften, replaced by small smiles of hope.

No one could feel down for long around John Birch. If John was in charge, things had a way of working out. But little did anyone realize how one American missionary, no matter how capable, might change the course of the Second World War.

For the American troops in the Pacific, morale, not money, had been a problem since Pearl Harbor. After many defeats, a retaliatory raid was now in progress hundreds of miles away in the airspace over Tokyo, led by pilot Lieutenant Colonel James H. Doolittle.

The plan would test the technical limits of the military as well as the skill and fortitude of the personnel involved. From the aircraft carrier USS *Hornet*, situated hundreds of miles from Japan in the Pacific, sixteen B-25 Mitchell bombers were to be launched from the flight deck for the first time. Never before had medium-sized warplanes been launched from a carrier—and they would not be able to return. Because of the planes' size and the limitations of their fuel tanks, the pilots would be forced to land at airfields in eastern China, landing strips that had been predetermined and approved. If all went well, the pilots were expected to make their way to Burma for further orders. The pilots did not have to be told that there was always the chance they might be captured by the Japanese and taken as prisoners of war.

On the morning of April 18, 1942, with Lt. Col. Doolittle in the first plane, the American fighters took off, despite bad weather and rough seas. Along with the weather, another "glitch" had complicated matters in the days before takeoff. A Japanese ship had been spotted near where the *Hornet* was supposed to have been, threatening the feasibility of the mission. Instead of launching the bombers four hundred miles from the coast of Japan, Doolittle and his fleet would now take off seven hundred miles from their destination.

The planes began launching bombs over Japan at an altitude of fifteen hundred feet, known as treetop level, successfully hitting military installation targets in Kobe, Yokohama, Nagoya, and Tokyo. The mission completed, Doolittle and crew, and the fifteen other planes, made their way for the airfields of China.

But the weather had taken a turn for the worse and visibility was poor. As Doolittle struggled to find the airstrip, he kept a close eye on his fuel tank. In these conditions he would never be able to land. There was only one option: He would have to bail out before the plane crashed. An experienced pilot, Doolittle had served as a flight instructor during World War I, besides being the first man to fly across the United States in less than a day, a feat he accomplished in 1922. The procedure was nothing new; only the terrain was foreign to him. In the thickening clouds, Doolittle and his crew jumped into near oblivion.

That day, all sixteen planes would be lost. In the weeks and months that followed, the fate of the bombers' personnel would read as follows: Seven men were injured, three were killed, and eight were taken prisoner by the Japanese. In the hours after the raid, though, the radios were silent. The whereabouts of the commanding officer and his crew were unknown.

From Kiangsi Province, John and the Chinese missionary traveled northeast by water into the province called Chekiang. They had borrowed a boat and traveled at times that were considered safest. From Sing Teng in Chekiang Province, the native brother would have a short trip to Shanghai. Before bidding him good-bye, John pressed some extra bills into his pocket. He had enough to survive for a while and he knew his needs were simple. Not too many missionaries could say they had lived on two dollars a month for several months in a row.

On the way back to Shangrao, John had thought of many places to stop. There were several country churches that could use some encouragement. But after visiting a few and being repeatedly warned of the dangers nearby, he was soon back on the river. At this point in his journey he was in a kind of no-man's land, or so this area near the western border of Chekiang Province was known. Still, he needed to eat, and so, in the early evening hours of this late April day, after spotting a small restaurant near the riverbank, John secured the boat and climbed the low cliff. The establishment was like so many in the backwaters of rural China, a simple place that served good and cheap native food.

Traveling in and out of Japanese-occupied areas since the start of the war had caused John to alter his appearance. John, who was short for an American man but the same height as many Chinese, could easily blend in with a crowd when dressed in the style of a rural Chinese man. To complete the disguise, he dyed his normally reddish-brown hair black and kept his face hidden by a hat. Close up, his blue eyes identified him as a foreigner. But from a distance at the restaurant, he could be any local villager. He ordered his rice and fish in the native dialect. He ate with chopsticks.

As he was eating, a Chinese man brushed against him, as if on his way out of the restaurant. "If you are an American, please follow me," he said quietly.

John finished his rice, so as not to call attention to himself, and followed the man. He was standing by a covered boat. With a slight motion of his hand, the missionary was directed inside.

In seconds, John was face-to-face with Lt. Col. James H. Doolittle and his beleaguered but smiling flight crew. He recognized the famous pilot immediately and just as quickly assessed the situation, even though he had heard nothing about the bombing raid. Sympathetic Chinese citizens had brought the downed pilot this far. Now those involved had turned to an American who by providence had wandered into this humble establishment. To John, there was no question he would risk his life to help get these Americans to safety. One thing was sure: They could not remain in no-man's land any longer. To capture a prize such as Doolittle, or any of his crew, would be a major coup for itinerant Japanese soldiers observed in the region. With a plan developing in his head, John apologetically introduced himself.

Seemingly at ease, Doolittle chuckled. "Son, what part of the South are you from?"

John Birch was only too happy to tell him.

TWO

His accent was of the South, but John Birch didn't cross the Mason-Dixon Line until he was twelve years old. The first memories he had of childhood centered around a fruit farm in Vineland, New Jersey, where his mother was raised. Nevertheless, his parents had regaled him with stories of the missing years, stories that had planted seeds of a missionary future.

John Morrison Birch was born on May 28, 1918, outside Allahabad, India, where his parents were both working as Presbyterian missionaries. In fact, George S. Birch and Ethel Ellis Birch had been in Allahabad only six months when John was born—but that did not seem to hinder their work at the Ewing Christian College. There, John's father, a graduate of the University of Georgia, taught agriculture and ran the college dairy, and his mother, a graduate of the College of Wooster in Wooster, Ohio, taught English and was instrumental in starting Bible classes for women.

Although he could trace his family lineage back to the Plymouth Colony (he was a direct descendant of John

Alden), and while he might boast to a few classmates that he was a relative of both Calvin Coolidge *and* Buffalo Bill Cody, John was intrigued with the Asian world. Indeed, whenever he thought of Allahabad, John conjured up two images. One was of a rare photograph of himself perched on the broad shoulders of his father, the two apparently out for a stroll in the city. John is wearing a playful triform hat, his blond curls peeking out from underneath, and his father is dressed to deliver a lecture at the college, looking businesslike in his collared shirt and tie. The other was of the beautiful fabrics his mother brought home with her to New Jersey, relics of a place that would always seem enchanting and otherworldly. Those fabrics, though, belied a truth John's parents had mentioned over and over again. India, with its dominant Hindu culture, was a place in desperate need of the gospel of Jesus Christ.

Allahabad, situated at the junction of the Yamuna and Ganges rivers, was both an important trading center and one of the oldest and holiest cities in all of India. In fact, thousands of Hindus flocked to the city each year to worship at the Great Mosque (the Jama Masjid). John liked to think that his father reached the Indian students from a practical perspective, showing them modern techniques to improve their quality of life, while his mother sought more to change their spiritual outlook, starting and attending as many Bible studies as she could handle. As one missionary in China, John hoped he could be both practical and spiritual, pitching in wherever necessary and praying, like the apostle Paul, without ceasing.

In 1920 the family, which now numbered two young sons, John and his infant brother, Ellis, sailed back to the United States. The move back was necessitated by George Birch's health, which had been slowly and steadily deteriorating since the couple had arrived in India, the result of malaria. However, once in New Jersey, George and his family seemed to thrive on what George described as "plain living and high thinking." Amid the rolling green hills and plentiful orchards of southern New Jersey, the young but growing family had the space to expand, and expand they did. John may have been one of two children when he arrived, but when they departed ten years later, he was one of seven young Birches.

Ethel's father was the owner of Blue Spruce Farms, a successful venture, and George soon became his father-in-law's partner. His agricultural expertise, as well as his work ethic, was a boon for the business. John, too, experienced success, but of a different sort. At the local grammar school he gained a reputation as an extremely gifted student. When he left the school, he was first in his class, a trend that was destined to continue.

Although academic achievement was prized in this family of educators, George and Ethel were most committed to raising their young family in a way that honored God. Family devotions were held every evening after dinner, and Sundays were devoted to the local Presbyterian church for worship and Sunday school. However, when a new minister was hired who conformed to a more "modernist" philosophy, the Birches pulled up spiritual stakes and found a new church home at the more fundamentalist West Baptist Church. George and Ethel, who quickly became Baptists, were thrilled when John at age seven came forward to the front of the church and made his own declaration of faith.

As a new Christian, John became especially interested in attending services where missionaries would be speaking. When he was eleven years old, he was in the audience at West Baptist when Leonard Livingstone Legters spoke of his encounter with Indian tribes in southern Brazil. As

Legters described a death wail that made his hair stand on end, the sound made when an Indian died and, supposedly, according to tribal custom, his spirit had been captured by demons, John hung on every word. A few days later John's parents found a note he had written: "The Lord is calling me to the mission field. I have the answer to the death wail of the lost."

In 1930, in the shadow of the Depression, John's father was offered a teaching position at Berry College in Mt. Berry, Georgia. The insecurity of the times threatened the fruit farm, and George, not wanting to be a burden to his wife's family, decided to accept the offer. Besides, he and Ethel were not strangers to the school. Before leaving for India, the couple had taught there for a few years and had in fact met each other there. Still, a teaching job was no guarantee of prosperity in those difficult days. George and Ethel, and every member of their brood, would have to cut corners in creative ways for the family to survive.

Thinking about his most recent crisis with money in Shangrao, John remembered vividly the hardships of life on the family's rented farm in Floyd County, Georgia. There was a time when all nine of them existed on five dollars a month for several months, and a time when stale bread dipped in milk was their only source of sustenance. Then there were the frequent crises of how to clothe seven children so they looked presentable for school. The strong faith of his parents, instilled in each one of the children, was the backbone of their existence, John realized, his eyes welling with tears as he thought about those times.

After a dispute about chaperoning school dances—as new fundamentalist Baptists, the Birches were adamantly against dancing—George left Berry and found another job as principal of a country grammar school. The new position required the family to move again, and at the same time, Ethel returned to teaching, finding a job at a local high school in the English department. The absence of mother and father left eldest son John in charge of the family, but in his early teens, he was more than up to the challenge, as his family soon discovered. Even though he was a full-time student at Gore High School in Chattooga County, he still did more than his share of chores. He also made sure that not one of his brothers or sisters missed any school except when they were sick. And, as usual, John soon found himself first in his class and the valedictorian.

Besides the typical childhood dreams and aspirations, John had one hope that lifted him above his often depressing living situation. This hope even had a name to go with it—Birchwood. Acres and acres of rich Georgia soil, around six hundred to be exact, were just waiting for him and his family, if only they could find a way to move there. Even though he was a young man, John had a strong attachment to the land of one's ancestors, land that a man wouldn't mind pouring his heart and soul into so his family might have a place to call their own. Like many Southerners before him, he was a kindred spirit who felt with all his being that land was worth fighting for, and worth dying for, too. In 1935, the Birches arrived at Birchwood, thanks largely to John. John licked his lips as he thought of the best way to describe the experience to Lt. Col. Doolittle and his crew.

Picture Birchwood, once my great-granddad's farm, if you will. Hundreds of acres, most of it woods, with the mighty Ocmulgee River running right through the property. There was plenty of land to work, though, and God knows my dad knew a thing or two about farming.

So, you say, why didn't we just move to Birch-wood right away? Well, after my great-grandpa was killed during the Civil War, Granddad was left with a share of the property, a share that had no house on it at the time—and that share was passed down to my father. But right next to his land was property owned by a granite quarry and a house, too, where the super-intendent of the quarry lived. When the quarry com-pany decided to sell the land (and the house, though it wasn't any bargain), they offered the property to us at a price we somehow could afford.

And what a house it is! There isn't a neighbor for miles—that could be the best part. Then there's a big old winding driveway leading up the hill to the house, and you're thinking as you're going up the road, this is some plantation or something. Well, that would be a gross misstatement, but you have to use your imagination of what could be. The house is really in a beautiful setting, with trees and bushes all around it, and gently sloping hills that run right down to the river. Even today, the house is still a work in progress, and it's still my dream. . .but that's getting ahead of the story.

Suffice it to say that in 1934 the decision was made to move there. I had just finished high school and this was surely more important than rushing right into college. Besides, what money we had I felt belonged to Birchwood. Other than what's owed to God, I still feel that way.

It was about a hundred miles from where we were living to Birchwood, which is near the city of Macon. My brother Ellis and I decided we would be in charge of the move since Dad was still teach-ing and couldn't leave for a year. In my head I had planned it all out. We had some head of cattle and we determined they should move first, why I'm not sure now. So Ellis and I, in a Model T, rode to Birchwood to begin building a corral. For the next few days we worked until we dropped and let out a whoop when the trailer truck containing the cattle arrived. By that time my younger brothers and sisters were at Birchwood, too, and they were given the responsibility of letting the cattle out each day to graze and watching them. No sheep dogs for the Birches, only children!

The corral done, we then set our minds to enclosing all the property. I'm talking about fencing four hundred acres all by ourselves. Here comes the big moment. When Daddy pulled up at Birchwood the next summer, Ellis and I couldn't stop grinning, we were so proud.

For the next few years, everything else seemed almost like a letdown. Daddy started in farming full-time and I entered Mercer University in Macon. But by my senior year, I knew what I wanted to do before I returned someday to Birchwood. God was calling me to the mission field, just like He had called Mama and Daddy years before. So I let myself be led.

THREE

When John and Lt. Col. Doolittle and his crew parted ways, they were well into Free China. They had traveled by sampan and then across the country by foot to get this far. After a firm handshake and profound thanks, Doolittle and company boarded a train that would take them to Chungking in Sichuan Province where there was an American army mission base. Before leaving, Doolittle promised to drop a line to John's parents and to mission headquarters saying that their son and missionary was alive and well. Then John waited for his train back to Shangrao.

John wasn't worried that he hadn't completed his accidental "mission," but he was concerned for the well-being of the heralded pilot. Far from viewing the bombing raid over Tokyo as a success, Doolittle was convinced that he would be court-martialed upon returning to the United States. After all, sixteen planes had been lost in a mission that was meant to lift morale, not sink the military into a deeper morass. Although John had no knowledge of the outcome at that time, he was later to discover that Doolittle's worries were needless.

First and foremost, the raid unnerved the Japanese government, which had assumed their home islands were safe from attack. In the months that followed, when Japan attempted to capture other islands in the Pacific, the efforts were thwarted by the United States Navy, which had a strong presence there. For his part in the raid, Doolittle was promoted to brigadier general and awarded the Congressional Medal of Honor. In the coming months, he would be assigned the command of American aviation forces that were destined to invade North Africa.

The rickety rhythm of the train was oddly soothing to the tired missionary. As the locomotive lurched east, John found comfort in the rural countryside. The low hills, where coal was mined, as well as kaolin clays used in the manufacture of porcelain, and fertile lowlands that followed, where peasants stood knee-deep in rice paddies, reminded John of home. He had probably bored Doolittle to death with all those stories of Birchwood, he thought to himself. Of course, he had told the pilot that he was a Baptist missionary in Shangrao, but he had skimmed over his seminary training and early years in China. Anyway, Doolittle was more impressed with John's language skills than his Christian faith. Bowing his head and closing his eyes, John silently thanked God for leading them to safety. Only God could have blessed him with the ability to speak Chinese dialects with a fluency possessed by few Westerners, which was key to their safe passage.

Maybe he had skimmed over the last few years because he had rushed headlong into his missionary assignment, rarely stopping to think about the abbreviated route he had taken to get there. Even though his encounter with the South American missionary when he was a child had influenced his career choice, it was during his final year at Mercer University that the decision to go to China was actually made. In January 1939, when J. Frank Norris conducted revival meetings at a church in southern Georgia, John was in the audience. Norris, a fiery preacher who was serving as pastor of First Baptist in Fort Worth, Texas, was the editor of the weekly Baptist publication, *The Fundamentalist*. The first night John attended he felt the Holy Spirit touch his heart with the need to put God first in his life. The second night, when Norris preached about the work of missionaries in China, John responded to the call by going to the front of the church to speak with the preacher himself.

"I'm willing to go," John said to Norris.

Norris's response was two words: "Write me."

John did. From Mercer University, where he graduated magna cum laude—and first in his class—with a bachelor's degree in 1939, John entered Norris's Fundamental Baptist Bible Institute in Fort Worth, Texas, where he was a member of the seminary's inaugural class. The school, which would change its name in succeeding years (Bible Baptist Seminary in 1952; Arlington Baptist College in 1973), was founded by the pastor and Dr. Louis Entzminger with the express purpose of teaching and training missionaries, Christian workers, and ministers. In the same year (1939), Norris and Dr. C. P. Staley formed the foreign mission agency known as the World Fundamental Baptist Missionary Fellowship that would serve as a natural extension of the college.

John had lived at home on the farm while attending Mercer, but in seminary he was forced to live in the bustling downtown area of Fort Worth. Because this was the first year students were accepted for full-time study at the seminary, all classes were held at the First Baptist Church, which was nestled amid the towering brick buildings. (In the next few years an entire campus would be constructed downtown, including, after 1945, a building to be named John Birch Hall.)

Observing the vast stretches of farmland out the train window, John couldn't contemplate living in a big city ever again. Perhaps because of his aversion to metropolitan life, John threw himself into studying, working twice as hard as most of his classmates—except perhaps his roommate, Oscar Wells, and one other young man. Of the seminary's first class of thirty, only the three of them would graduate after one year.

By far the best thing about campus life for a boy used to close relationships forged among a big, loving family was Oscar Wells. Besides a strong Christian faith, the two shared the same dream of one day serving in China. Their motivation became even stronger after Norris informed them in January 1940 that refugees by the thousands were crowding into the city of Shanghai. Fred and Lois Donnelson, who were among the fifteen missionaries sponsored by Norris's missionary fellowship and serving in Shanghai, had reported they didn't have a sanctuary big enough to seat everyone. Together, John and Oscar informed Dr. Norris they wanted to go, despite the fellowship's lack of funds. By April, however, both young men had raised enough money to make the trip. Both were eager to fulfill their destiny.

On June 10, 1940, John, Oscar, and Ralph Van Northwick received their diplomas from the institute, having completed the two-year program in half the time. At the ceremony all three graduates preached short sermons, and John's topic was the inspiration of the Bible. Once again, John had graduated first in his class. After a brief vacation at Birchwood, John and Oscar returned to Fort Worth for a proper send-off by the First Baptist Church. A month later, under the auspices of the World Fundamental Baptist Missionary Fellowship, the two young seminarians sailed for Shanghai.

To the young American missionaries, the bustling hub situated near the mouth of the Yangtze, which poured into the East China Sea, was a bold introduction to everything Chinese. Several million residents crowded into the port city on the Huangpu River that had started as a fishing village more than a thousand years earlier. By the eighteenth century, Shanghai, a name that means "on the sea," had become a center of fabric and garment production, and now, well into the twentieth, was a mecca for culture and the arts. The city had even gained the reputation, much to the disdain of many Chinese, as the "Paris of the East."

To many Westerners the weather in Shanghai was the first stumbling block, but John, accustomed to the stifling summers of Georgia, didn't seem too affected by the humid conditions. July was the hottest month and, after June, the wettest one. Typhoons were also known to occur during the summer months.

Glad to be ashore, John and Oscar soon joined the throngs of passengers hoping for a breeze as they walked along the Huangpu waterfront on a boulevard known as the Bund. The Bund was also the name of Shanghai's international settlement and a symbol of the dreaded foreign domination that had surfaced during the Opium Wars of the nineteenth century. A major thoroughfare, the Bund was home to trolley cars and automobiles, the latter often having to swerve to avoid hitting bicycles and pedestrians. They passed a small park and soon entered the British district, dominated by the Customhouse, the British Consulate, and foreign and Chinese banks. Since 1843 Shanghai had been home to a British colony, a development resisted by the Chinese but forced upon them by the Treaty of Nanking, the result of the Opium Wars. The British were soon followed by the French and Americans, who all found refuge in territorial zones inside the city.

In preparation for his missionary service in China, John had studied history, becoming most familiar with the turbulent events of the twentieth century. He was well aware that Shanghai was currently under siege from a different war. Since 1937 the city had been occupied by the Japanese, and by 1939 Japan had much of eastern China in its grip. But how could such a small country have taken the initiative to seize such a behemoth as China? The answer, John knew, lay in the wrenching civil war that had been plaguing China since the 1920s.

After the turmoil of the Boxer Uprising in the early twentieth century, the reins of power in the government were held by regional warlords who had come to power as military leaders. A new government emerged in the early 1920s when Sun Yat-sen organized the Guomindang (Kuomintang) or Nationalist Party. At the same time, to challenge the authority of Sun Yat-sen, the Communist Party was formed, eventually to be led by Mao Tse-tung. Chaos ensued when Sun died in 1925 and leadership of the Guomindang fell to Chiang Kai-shek, who immediately began purging the party of Communists. Before his death, Sun had allowed Communists to join the Nationalist party individually but not as a bloc. This purging was followed by the organized slaughter of Communists living in Shanghai, Canton, and Nanking. In 1928 civil war between the two parties erupted, a crisis that would not be resolved until 1949 when Mao assumed control of China, and Chiang and the Nationalists were forced to retreat to the island of Taiwan.

In 1931, when China was suffering not only the ill effects of war but also widespread famine, including disease decimating the population, Japan, led by Prime Minister Baron Tanaka, seized the two northernmost provinces of China. Tanaka, who was consumed by religious fervor, had declared only a year earlier that the whole world would become Shinto worshipers—followers of the principal religion of Japan—and China would be the first step toward that end. While foreigners, including missionaries, had once been despised in China and considered a threat, John and his fellow passengers felt relatively safe in 1940 in Japanese-occupied Shanghai. Japan did not want to jeopardize its position in China or invite intervention by Western nations, at least not yet. For the native Chinese, though, the Japanese occupation meant years of living in terror. Thousands were driven from their homes and gang rapes were common. Often the only safe retreat would be in the homes of foreigners or in mission schools or hospitals.

Still, the threat of war was in the air, and even the United States, though not at war with Japan as yet, was issuing warnings through the State Department to United States citizens to evacuate China. That warning certainly applied to Fred and Lois Donnelson, as well as Mrs. Josephine Sweet (known as "Mother Sweet"), who nonetheless welcomed John and Oscar with open arms. From 1932 to 1937 the Donnelsons and Mother Sweet had worked in Hangchow, coming to Shanghai only when the war had given them no other option, going home not being one for them. All three were deeply committed to serving in China for life. Mother Sweet herself had served as a missionary in China for forty years, even returning to the field after the death of her husband. Now health issues prevented her from venturing out of Shanghai.

The Donnelsons' church in Shanghai was flourishing beyond belief, and John and Oscar could only shake their heads at the statistics Fred provided. In the three years they had been there, Fred and Lois had baptized more than a thousand Chinese, with new converts coming every week. "Every Sunday, the church is filled to capacity," Fred said, as he showed the two men to their rooms in a missionary house near the church. "And during the week we have evangelistic meetings every night, too. You boys have certainly come to help us at the right time!"

Still, that first night, after meeting Mother Sweet and hearing her stories about war-torn Hangchow, John could think of nothing else. He needed to be out in the field, risking his life to proclaim the gospel of Jesus Christ. Realistically, though, he knew he couldn't convince a single soul of the Christian faith until he learned the Chinese language. Once that hurdle was crossed, though, there would be no stopping him—war or no war.

Just as he had thrown himself into his studies in seminary and excelled in every academic venue since childhood, John devoted himself to learning the Chinese language, becoming fairly proficient within four months. To succeed as a missionary, it was imperative that he learn the language spoken by the vast majority of Chinese, or Han, people.

The task was daunting. Like the Romance languages, which share many common characteristics, the Sino-Tibetan languages (including Chinese, Tibetan, and other tribal languages) have many similar features. Unfortunately, John thought when he began his study, there were few similarities between the two groups. Chinese is a monosyllabic language that is spoken using different tones to convey meaning. A high or low pitch says one thing, while a moving pitch (going higher or lower) means something entirely different. The Chinese indeed have a singsong way of speaking.

Then there are the regional dialects. Mandarin is the most popular dialect, but there are six other dialect groups as well. John had heard of the Cantonese, or Yue, dialect, spoken in Hong Kong, but he was unfamiliar with the Gan and Wu dialects, which he had to learn as well. Fortunately, those who spoke Mandarin, Gan, or Wu had the ability to understand each other since the dialects were similar. In Kiangsi Province where Shangrao was located, Gan was used by most of the people, whereas in Chekiang Province, Wu was the dialect of choice.

Besides the dialects, the rudiments of Chinese are often confusing. Verb tenses are never given, and a string of modifiers often precedes the subject in a sentence. Furthermore, subject and verb do not have to agree with each other. If John hadn't been so determined, the language might have defeated him early on.

By Thanksgiving, John was ready to put his schooling into practice. He would still have to return to Shanghai for periodic language exams, but he had made remarkable progress. Anyway, he had a reason to leave. Pastor Du of the Tai Ben Fang Church in Hangchow—the church started by Mother Sweet and her husband—had invited John to teach at the church's Bible school. Hangchow, which was the capital of Chekiang Province, was about one hundred miles from Shanghai. Like Shanghai, Hangchow had been occupied by the Japanese since 1937. But unlike picturesque Shanghai, Hangchow was a shadow of its former self, its population having been reduced to 200,000 and many of its buildings nothing more than rubble from the bombings. By December, Hangchow was in the middle of a famine situation, torn between the Japanese forces occupying the city and Chiang's armies outside trying to recapture it.

On Christmas Day, John preached his first sermon in the Tai Ben Fang Church and fifteen people came forward to accept Jesus Christ. Even though John was pleased, Pastor Du had placed a concern in his heart for the rural churches outside Hangchow, many of which he was afraid were no longer in existence. Braving blizzards and the ever-present Japanese soldiers, John and various Chinese pastors made two trips in January, each time venturing farther afield. By the end of the month they had a new goal: to go all the way to Shangrao, in Kiangsi Province, where they wanted to encourage what remained of a Baptist church that Fred Donnelson had once started.

A friend's visit would be a good excuse for a mission trip, reasoned John. It had been months since he had seen Oscar, and he was thrilled to receive his telegram that he would be visiting Hangchow. When John had left after Thanksgiving, Oscar had remained with the Donnelsons in Shanghai, having made slower progress in his language study. Staying behind had not been without benefit, though, as Oscar had proceeded to meet and court his future wife, Myrtle, and now a late June wedding was planned.

"Up for a little trip?" John queried his former room-mate, his blue eyes brighter than usual.

Oscar had been around this Georgia boy long enough to know the power of Southern understatement. And he had certainly heard the story—several times!—of the fencing of Birchwood. But Oscar was a missionary through and through and his heart started beating faster at the prospect of an adventure for the Lord. "Sure, John. That's why I'm here," he said convincingly.

Riding out of Hangchow a few days later on bicycles,

the three missionaries (including Pastor Du) waved to the Japanese soldiers as if they were off to enjoy a picnic. After that, the next few days were a blur to Oscar and John as the three of them, led by Pastor Du, navigated waterways and trudged through forests, always traveling at night and sleeping by day. Finally, two hundred miles and several days later, they arrived in Shangrao.

They found the church intact, but most of the men in Shangrao had gone to fight in the Chinese army. After preaching to a small congregation of forty, the missionaries were encouraged to go to other villages where there were no churches. John knew after a few such visits that he could not ignore God's call any longer. He and Pastor Du had to return to Hangchow and Oscar to Shanghai, but he could come back and use Shangrao as his base for evangelization— someday. Somehow God would provide a way.

FOUR

In late April, the train carrying John "home" from his rescue of Lt. Col. Doolittle pulled into the Shangrao station. He was glad to be back with his Chinese friends and glad to be "in the field" working again for the Lord. However, when he reached the post office to see what had arrived for him, there were two telegrams waiting. One concerned money that would be sent to him from the mission office. The other, from the American military mission in Chungking, ordered him to report immediately for duty at the Ch'u Hsien airbase, and to go from there northwest to Chungking.

A military order of a different kind brought me to Shangrao, he thought to himself. *Odd that one from my own country now forces me to leave.* Yet in his heart he knew that there are no oddities with God and no such thing as coincidence.

On December 8, 1941, the day following Japan's attack on the United States at Pearl Harbor, an order for John's arrest was issued. The order was to be carried out by a Japanese detachment in Hangchow. John, who had been semiofficially in Shangrao since September, had returned in early December for another language exam in Shanghai and then gone on to Hangchow to preach to a regiment of Chinese soldiers. Although he had been encouraged to stay in Hangchow for a few days, he was more than aware of what he called a "gathering gloom" around him. Traveling by boat, he went west to Kiangsi Province and to the town of Shangrao, narrowly missing being captured by Japanese soldiers.

Now that Shangrao was his home base, John and Chinese missionaries Chen and Hu began evangelizing in the rural areas of the province where there had been no Christian message for more than ten years. On one excursion they bicycled to Hwang Ho where they preached to more than a hundred people and where forty accepted Jesus Christ. Another time they traveled to the town of Shia Chi where years earlier an aged town elder had stood alone, preaching his faith to Chinese Communists and narrowly avoiding execution. He had waited a long time to be baptized and now, finally, John made the trip to his home. Another time, on a drill field where three hundred Chinese soldiers were training, John, Chen, and Hu preached and offered a call to come to the Lord. At first only a few stood, but after a few minutes, all the men wanted to accept Jesus as their Savior. John was overcome with a joy he had never known.

Writing to his family in Georgia, John described his months in Shangrao:

> Free China is rightly named—what a glorious liberty to preach the gospel is mine! I can get on my bicycle and ride to Chungking, to Kunming, Rangoon, Burma, Siberia, Tibet, India, and Turkestan! But I

*don't need to go so far—within one hundred miles of
Shangrao there are hundreds of towns and villages
without the gospel and hundreds of thousands of souls
who have not even heard the message of salvation. . . .
What a privilege is mine! May I use it rightly.*[1]

Even though he had been safe in Shangrao for the last
few months, he again had that sense of doom. It was only a
matter of time before the Japanese occupied all of Kiangsi
Province. Moreover, lately he was torn by the need to serve
his country instead of serving God in the mission field.
With his finances in such a precarious state prior to the
Chinese army order issued in late April, he had surmised
that God might be leading him elsewhere. On April 13,
1942, he wrote the following to the American military mission at Chungking:

*I am writing to enquire as to the present oppor-
tunities for and the need of volunteer service in the
United States armed forces in this part of the world.*

*I am an American citizen. . .first honor man,
Mercer University. . .and an independent Baptist
missionary. . . . Since that time [December 8, 1941]
I. . .am finding [preaching] increasingly hard to do on
an empty stomach (no word or funds from home since
November).*

*To continue my self-glorification, I can preach
and pray, both in English and Chinese, can speak
enough Mandarin to get by, can build and operate
radio transmitters and receivers, can stand physical
hardship. I believe in God, His Son, in America, and
in freedom; I hold them all more precious than peace
and more precious than my earthly life. . . .*

> *I should like to be a chaplain—I am an ordained*
> *Baptist minister. . .but if there is no demand for chap-*
> *lains I should cheerfully tote a rifle, run a shortwave*
> *set, or drive a truck, or be an interpreter, or whatever*
> *they tell me to do. What pay does a private draw a*
> *month? Twenty-one dollars? That's more than enough*
> *for me. Please write me what my chances would be if*
> *I were to go to Chungking to volunteer, even if you*
> *have to write "Nil."*[2]

This new order to go to the airbase and then to Chung-king was God's way of saying there was more for him to do in China than surrender to the Japanese. Undoubtedly, Doolittle had told the American military about him, he thought. They probably needed a chaplain at the airbase and one at Chungking as well. Pleased with his conclusion, he knew at last he would be serving his country as well as his God.

The morning he was to leave he began his devotionals in the Book of Luke. Near the end of the twelfth chapter, though, his breath seemed to catch in his throat. One verse had caught his attention. "For unto whomsoever much is given, of him shall be much required: and to whom men have committed much, of him they will ask more" (Luke 12:48).

On May 4, 1942, John wrote to his parents from Ch'u Hsien airbase: "This week I have been serving as chaplain to the fly-ers who bombed Tokyo; now most of them have gone on to Chungking, and when the dead and wounded shall have been cared for, I shall go on, too. Needless to say, please pray."[3]

When he left less than a month later, on that very day, the Japanese bombed the airbase where he had been serving unofficially as chaplain, killing four people. A pattern was emerging for the American missionary, one he wasn't sure how to analyze. Just after he and the other Chinese preachers had left Shangrao, the Japanese captured their mission, part of their conquest of the entire Kiangsi Province. There was no turning back.

Because of the advancing Japanese troops, John's journey to Chungking became nothing short of circuitous. From Ch'u Hsien he finally hitched a ride on a gasoline truck bound for southern Kiangsi Province, not exactly the direction he wanted to travel. He had been told, though, that there was an army airfield there and possibly he could "hitch" a ride to Chungking. Floods and washed-out bridges prevented him from proceeding immediately. On June 10, he finally headed west to Hunan Province and from there caught a train taking him to Kweilin, in Kuangsi Province. He was still more than three hundred miles from Chungking.

Safe for a time from the threat of being captured, John felt more at ease in Kweilin than he had earlier on his journey. The city was home to the southernmost Chinese airbase, forming a sort of triangle with Kunming to the west and Chungking to the north. Once in Kweilin he managed to find a ride to the airfield and soon was face-to-face with one of the most legendary American commanders in China: Brigadier General Claire Lee Chennault.

Chennault was called "Colonel" or "the Old Man" by his devoted men and "the Big Tiger" by the Chinese, whose love for him bordered on adoration. To the missionary John Birch, there was no disputing that with his lined face and jutting chin, the general was a formidable, chain-smoking presence. When John introduced himself and told of his orders to go to Chungking, Chennault narrowed his eyes and gave him a more thorough once-over.

"You wouldn't be the missionary who rescued Doolittle and his crew?" he asked gruffly.

"Yes, sir," answered John, his eyes never wavering from the general.

"Doolittle asked you to come to Chungking?"

"Not exactly, sir. I'm hoping to serve as a chaplain at the base there."

Chennault threw his cigarette to the ground and ground it into the dirt with his boot. "Well, I've already got one chaplain, but I could use someone with your skills, if I know anything about you. You know the Chinese, the people, how to speak the language. Think about it. I'm taking off in an hour. Glad to give you a ride."

Three weeks later, in Chungking, John reported directly to Chennault—in a role he was well suited to play. He would still be a missionary, in that he would never stop sharing the gospel if given the opportunity. From now on, though, he would be recognized as an intelligence officer in the United States Armed Forces.

FIVE

It was all Doolittle's doing, with a little prompting by General Chennault, but John was well suited to his new position in army intelligence. Yes, he could speak several Chinese dialects fluently, but he also had a working knowledge of operating a radio, as well as uncommon mental and physical fortitude, attributes he himself had listed in his initial letter to the army base. If anything, he owed his new career to his years at Birchwood, though no one in the army was aware of that.

When he and Ellis moved into the old family homestead, they had decided to build their own radio. What they lacked in money John possessed in mechanical ability. As an intelligence officer, John would be asked to put that knowledge to use, and then some. Radio was an essential element in conveying information, and John would have to be able to operate a system in the most adverse conditions.

Upon his arrival in Chungking, John went through the usual channels to see if his request to be installed as an official chaplain had been approved. After two weeks of waiting,

John learned that he could not be considered because he had not graduated from an accredited seminary. (He had been in the first class at the Fort Worth seminary and accreditation had not yet been granted.) Finding himself in limbo, he began to reconsider Chennault's offer, sketchy though it was. After further conversation with the general, he was offered a commission as a second lieutenant. If the army changed its mind on the chaplaincy requirement, the general said, John would be free to leave his command at any time.

On July 4, 1942, John Birch was inducted into the service as a second lieutenant and assigned to the China Air Task Force, the group formerly known as the American Volunteer Group (AVG). Although at first he was confused by the situation at Chungking, late-night conversations with a variety of military men finally filled in the blanks. The state of the command into which he was inducted was one consumed by drama, with the pivotal role being played by John Birch's commanding officer, Gen. Chennault.

His was a larger-than-life presence, to be sure. The officer, who hailed from Commerce, Texas, had come to China in 1937, shortly after the outbreak of the war with Japan. A retired major in the United States Air Force, he had come to help train Chinese pilots and act as an air advisor. He soon won authorization from Chiang Kai-shek to form the AVG, winning final approval from President Franklin Roosevelt in 1941. With such perks as double their military salary, plus bonuses for Japanese planes shot down, former U.S. military men were eager to be recruited for the AVG—until they realized the difficulties of their mission and the harshness of their taskmaster. Under the strict tutelage of Chennault, AVG pilots learned how to pilot P-40 Tomahawks, becoming particularly skilled in diving at extraordinary speeds and then retreating. They had to be good to avoid the more skilled Japanese pilots. In the weeks following the attack on Pearl Harbor, the AVG began putting its training to use. After seven months of combat, the AVG pilots, who had downed 297 Japanese planes, were known by the name given them by the Chinese—"Flying Tigers." There was no doubt they had given an important psychological edge to the American war effort.

Chennault was recalled to active duty in the Army Air Force in April 1942, and by July, the AVG was part of the military effort under a new name. But few of the former standout pilots wanted to remain on board. Most felt they deserved some recognition from their country and a well-earned leave to go home. Those who remained did so out of loyalty to Chennault. After all, the general would need help training the newest recruits, courtesy of Gen. Joe Stilwell, the commander of United States forces in the China-Burma-India theater. And therein lay the next element of this ongoing drama. Stilwell believed the war with Japan would be won on the ground, concentrating on Burma, while Chennault was committed to an air campaign and assisting Chiang Kai-shek. The conflict between the two men would, in fact, result in John's first intelligence assignment. Before he reached the general's office, John could hear the result of his commander's two-pack-a-day habit.

"Nasty bronchitis," Chennault said, in a hoarse voice that sounded like tires skidding on gravel.

"I'm sorry to hear that, sir," Birch replied.

"What did you say?" Chennault asked, stepping closer. All those years of flying in an open cockpit had greatly diminished the commander's hearing. Waving his hand to excuse John from speaking, the general continued. "Doesn't matter. Got a job for you, son. I want you to check on a few airfields for me."

"Can I preach in Chinese churches along the way?" John asked, not forgetting his original calling and the opportunities that might arise.

Chennault gave him a strange look. "I don't care what you do, as long as you do my job. Understood?"

John couldn't help smiling back. "When do I start?"

John's mission was deceptively simple, but exhausting. He was to locate several airfields in southeastern China where Chennault, on previous flying missions, had left caches of ammunition and fuel. Chennault wanted to make sure these caches were still there in the not-so-unlikely event the new China Air Task Force had to make emergency landings. In September John and a Chinese companion left Chungking, taking only what they could carry. They walked, hitchhiked, and flew in small planes to reach their destinations, covering over a thousand miles. At each airfield, John insisted on seeing each cache for himself, all the while taking detailed notes.

As a result of his first "mission," John made an excellent impression on his commander, as evidenced by a letter written to him by Gen. Chennault: "Your recent secret mission in relation to intelligence matters, which led you extremely close to enemy territory, has been invaluable to the China Air Task Force. The successful accomplishment of this hazardous mission required fortitude, courage, and devotion to duty. The excellent manner in which you have carried out this difficult duty is highly commended."[1]

By November, the task force had been ordered by Stilwell to move from Chungking to Kunming, a frontier outpost in Yunnan Province more than three hundred miles away, much to Chennault's distress. Chungking was the capital of Chiang's Nationalist government. Moving the Flying

Tigers all the way to Kunming was going to make it harder for Chennault to help China defeat Japan. Still, the general was determined to keep his planes flying—and his information up to date.

John was quickly dispatched to begin updating aerial maps, based on his mission to the various Chinese airfields. And as Christmas approached, he found a way to use his new position for the Lord. He was able to substitute for Chennault's chaplain at various worship services, as well as preach to American military men stationed at Kunming. He had come to enjoy the city of Kunming with its temperate climate and higher altitude. All too soon, John would be leaving on another adventure, this time behind enemy lines.

Chennault was becoming more concerned about intelligence on the eastern coast, particularly information about Japanese warships visible from the shoreline. Much like the intelligence-gathering operation that was taking place in Europe, the general wanted John to live behind enemy lines, reporting by radio the position of enemy ships. When John was informed of his new mission, he asked if he could preach to Chinese churches in the area. Again, he was given permission, provided he kept up his intelligence gathering.

John first flew to a small village on the coast, across the strait from Formosa (Taiwan). To conceal his identity from the ever-present Japanese, he assumed his former disguise as a poor countryman, dying his hair black and keeping his eyes hidden by wearing a hat. From there he employed Chinese coolies to help him transport his radio equipment in rented boats. One time John, who was alone, was forced to hide his radio inside a farm worker's basket that was used for manure. When he passed Japanese soldiers, they recognized the basket and held their noses, letting John go by without question. Finally, at a village on the coast where he could see the activities of Japanese boats, he set up a radio station. To run the station after he left, he hired two Christian fishermen whom he taught the radio code he had devised. They would now report back directly to Kunming, providing valuable information. Again for his work John received a commendation from Gen. Chennault.

The following March, the China Air Task Force became the 14th Air Force, to distinguish Chennault's group from the fighting going on in India and Burma. At the same time, the general, who was promoted to major general, was given five hundred more planes, and John, who had received his first lieutenant's silver bar, was given a new assignment, in an effort to squelch the recent spate of attacks by Japanese planes on Kunming and other cities. As a member of the 14th, he was to serve as liaison and intelligence officer with Marshal Hsueh Yo, commander of the Chinese Ninth War Area in Changsha, the capital of Hunan Province. Marshal Hsueh, held in high regard by Chennault, had been nicknamed "Little Tiger" by the Flying Tigers.

His intelligence information would help the 14th Air Force assist the Chinese forces fighting on the ground. He was to provide steady, reliable information—information that would be transmitted directly to the 14th's headquarters. His efforts, and his exploits, would not be easily forgotten.

SIX

John was given the house next door to Marshal Hsueh's headquarters as his residence in Changsha. Working closely with Marshal Hsueh and poring over maps together, John was able to determine pockets of Japanese guerrilla units. Again, to preserve his life and for the sake of his country, he would have to go undercover to obtain information. This time, dressed as a Chinese coolie, his radio equipment hidden in crude baskets, he would be accompanied by barefoot farm boys. They would have to walk or travel by horseback more than a hundred miles to reach the battlefront.

Climbing up a hill, the sounds of gunfire echoing around him, John found a patch of ground to begin transmitting information. Before finding his hideout, John had laid white strips of cloth not far from Japanese troops that he hoped would be visible to American pilots. Once he was on the air, John said, "White Pontiac, do you see my white panels?"

A crackling followed and then, miraculously, came a voice. "Roger."

John was less cryptic with his next message. "There's a

howitzer a quarter of a mile from the pagoda."

Again, the response, "Roger."

If the bombs missed the target, John was there to direct the pilot for one more try. This back-and-forth exchange of information went on for six weeks until there was a lull in the fighting and John returned to Changsha.

Commendations again were given to the brave missionary. John Birch was singled out for a reason: For the first time in history, an American had been able to live and work in the field with the Chinese army. No one, not even war correspondents, had ever accomplished this feat. John had established a precedent for intelligence gathering, and many former missionaries in China would follow his lead as the war progressed. When Gen. Chennault himself pinned the Legion of Merit medal on the missionary, he offered uncommon words of praise: "In a war theater where courage is commonplace, that of John Birch has proved exceptional."

About John Birch, Gen. Hsueh Yo said, "During the whole of this. . .campaign, the diligent and efficient service of First Lieutenant John M. Birch, liaison and intelligence officer. . . who has worked continuously day and night without taking rest, contributed greatly to the close cooperation of the ground and air troops and to the happy conclusion of the said campaign. It is requested that he be given high merits for his brilliant service."[1] To that glowing letter, which Gen. Chennault returned to John, the Big Tiger added these words: "Your successes will play an important part in finally driving the Japanese from China."

From Changsha John returned to Kunming for a new intelligence briefing. He was anxious to meet the new team that Gen. Chennault had assembled—among them, Arthur Hopkins, a Yale graduate whom John had met at Chungking; William Drummond, a former art dealer in

Peking; and Sergeant Leroy Eichenberry. A new mission was about to get under way, one that would push John to the limits of survival.

John was ordered to set up radio contacts along the Yangtze River, much as he had done on the eastern coast of China. The fighting was especially heavy in this region, and intelligence was of the utmost importance. He was to leave on his mission from Changsha, where Marshal Hsueh Yo was still stationed. Going with him from Kunming were two new intelligence agents, Hopkins and Eichenberry, who would be the new liaisons for Gen. Hsueh Yo.

As usual, John was accompanied by Chinese assistants, and as usual, the journey was difficult. After ten days, the party reached the Yangtze, mosquito-bitten but alive. John was the first American many of the Chinese fighters there had seen in years. On Chinese junks, he set out with his assistants down the Yangtze, setting up a total of five radio stations, one every hundred miles. Again, he found reliable men who learned his radio code and would be paid to transmit information back to Kunming. He also taught the Chinese fighters how to identify American planes flying closely overhead. On the way back, John had a close call with a unit of Japanese fighters and narrowly escaped with his life.

When he arrived back in Kunming, he was thinner than he had ever been, and his skin, which was burnished to a bronze, stretched tightly over his bones. To recover his strength, he ate two heaping platefuls at every meal and slept between meals. Physically, he was soon back to his former self, but emotionally, he needed a boost.

While at the army base, he received word that the family's home at Birchwood had burned to the ground, the result of errant sparks from a nearby freight train. No one was injured, but the family had no insurance and, therefore, little money to rebuild. Neighbors had been kind, and the Birches had managed to find a temporary place to live. John immediately wrote back this Bible verse: "Those things which cannot be shaken may remain" (Hebrews 12:27). For some time, he had been sending one hundred dollars each month from his army pay to his parents, telling them to buy land with it. Now he said, "Any land or money that is mine I here and now give to you, Father and Mother. Please sell anything else before your own land!"[2]

John had no idea when, if ever, he would return to Birchwood. He had been promoted to captain since his last mission, but commendations and honors were the furthest thing from his mind. He was desperately concerned about the progression of the war, especially the recent buildup of Japanese troops near Changsha. Gen. Hsueh Yo, whom John regarded as a friend, would not be able to withstand an attack of that magnitude without considerable help from Chennault's pilots. And, as usual, Chennault was engaged in his ongoing tug-of-war with Gen. Stilwell, unable to secure more aircraft.

Before leaving from Changsha on his next mission, John wrote his parents the following:

> *Beginning tomorrow I shall be unable to write you, so please don't be alarmed if there is a lapse in the arriving of my letters. Please continue to remember me in your prayers; if my hour to depart should strike, I am ready to go, thanks to the merit of our Savior, the Lord Jesus Christ. But I hope that God will give me yet further time to live for Him fruitfully here on this earth; I've wasted so much of His time already, living for self, that I really feel ashamed to ask for more.*[3]

In early May 1944 John left from Changsha to in-
filtrate a burgeoning pocket of Japanese troops stationed
to the northwest in Anhwei Province, in the area known
as the Yellow River (Huang He) plains. Traveling no more
than fifty miles a day, he finally arrived at the destination
on May 10, only to find that he could report few targets
to Kunming. The suffocating Japanese presence prevented
him from getting too close. What he was able to report the
Americans already knew: Japan was preparing for a huge of-
fensive, and Changsha was likely one of the targets.

It was in the pocket in Anhwei Province, where a
regiment of Chinese troops led by Gen. Wang had been
trapped for a few months, that John set up a central radio
station, as well as two airfields where planes could land
if they were in trouble. Eichenberry and Drummond
were with him in the pocket, helping set up the station.
Thousands of Chinese helped construct the airfields, even
building a small terminal and radio shack close to the
runway. The first plane to leave took Eichenberry back to
Kunming because he was ill with cholera, but John stuck
it out. As summer neared, he was not feeling well, either,
in the stifling heat.

He made one trip back to Kunming later in the summer for a much-needed rest but was soon back on the
Yellow River plains. The summer had seen the landing of
Allied troops at Normandy, as well as the fall of Changsha
to the Japanese, with Gen. Hsueh Yo's troops retreating.
Chennault's fighters had prevented the situation from becoming a total disaster, but how much longer the Chinese
could hang on in their present state was unknown. For
his part, John continued making small excursions to remote regions to send intelligence reports. He didn't have
to ask anymore if he could preach along the way. Now

he also carried his New Testament with him and a supply of gospel tracts to distribute.

Christmas 1944 brought the usual memories of Birchwood, but at the Anhwei pocket the last thing John and Drummond were expecting was guests, especially missionaries. They were Dutch, British, and American missionaries who had managed to survive the war because they were stationed in remote areas. Now, though, they had begun to fear for their lives. Somehow word had reached them about an airfield in Anhwei, and they arrived in waves in late December, hoping for a flight out of China.

When John radioed Kunming, he was told that the air force wasn't running a ferry service for missionaries. "But every day more arrive," he pleaded. Using their code term for the airfield, Drummond radioed to other stations, "Harvey's Restaurant is absolutely jammed. Please don't send any more customers." Finally, John decided the situation required dire measures. He wasn't going to lie, but he needed to rephrase the request. Radioing Kunming again, he said, "I have a packet of intelligence information that needs to go back to headquarters as soon as possible." He was told a plane would be coming.

Just as the plane was secured, though no date was given for arrival, they were almost snowed in. No plane would dare to land in these conditions, John told Gen. Wang, who was concerned about the plight of the missionaries. "How many men with shovels do you need to clear the runway? Eight hundred enough?"

Within hours the runway was cleared and all but one of the missionaries were able to leave, with the last one leaving a month later.

Change was in the air as the months of 1945 passed. In a

series of moves intended to snub Gen. Chennault, the 14th Air Force was reassigned to Chengtu from Kunming. Then, in a more direct hit, Chennault was passed over as overall commander of the air force in China. Finally, the Office of Strategic Services (OSS) was brought in to coordinate the intelligence operation, and John found himself reporting to a new commander.

These personnel moves likely signaled that the war was finally winding down. On May 8, 1945, the war ended in Europe, even though Japan continued to fight, though not with the same vengeance. What was becoming clear to John was that Japanese forces were retreating, and right behind them were the Chinese Communists, clearly preparing to take over when the war was over.

On July 4, 1945, John wrote home: "There is only one real problem in the world with all its complicated evils, and there is only one answer, amidst the maze of futile plans. Here is the problem and the answer: 'The wages of sin is death, but the free gift of God is eternal life through Jesus Christ our Lord'" (Romans 6:23).[4]

On July 8, Gen. Chennault requested retirement because of health reasons—but John knew better. In the Chinese custom, he was saving face. When he left China on August 1, 1945, hundreds of thousands of Chinese lined the streets of Chungking, even pushing his car all the way to the airport.

On August 6 and August 9, the United States dropped atomic bombs on Hiroshima and Nagasaki. By August 15 Japan had surrendered unconditionally, though the formal surrender aboard the U.S. battleship *Missouri* wouldn't take place until September 2. World War II was over, as was China's ongoing war with Japan, but China's civil war was far from settled.

SEVEN

Following the surrender of Japan, there was still intelligence work to be done in China. Chief among the duties for the OSS was going to the various Japanese bases and arranging for the official surrender to the proper authorities. It was important the United States reach these bases before the Chinese Communists could commandeer Japanese arms and equipment.

John was ordered to go to Hsuchow, in Shandong Province, about one hundred miles northeast of where he was currently stationed in Anhwei Province. The Japanese had installed a headquarters at Hsuchow, and word was that Communists had already infiltrated the surrounding area. The mission, while not as dangerous as others he had accepted, was still fraught with uncertainty. On the morning of August 20, John and his party of ten departed, with John as the commanding officer and Lieutenant Tung Fu-Kuan of the Chinese army as liaison officer.

By August 24, the group was on the train heading toward Hsuchow when it was reported there was a break in the tracks ahead. Upon securing a handcar on which to put their equipment, John and his party proceeded to a small station farther along, where there was a Japanese garrison. There they spent the night. The next morning they continued on, taking turns pushing the heavy handcar. At around noon, they met up with a force of Chinese Communists, which Lt. Tung estimated to be in the hundreds, that was tearing down telephone wires.

After being surrounded by the Communists, John went forward to speak with a man he assumed was the commanding officer. When he returned, he said they were allowed to proceed, but he was clearly troubled. The Communists had wanted him to give up all his equipment, but he had refused. Up ahead, John had been informed, were more Communist forces.

When they reached the second group, two Communist officers approached, and John and Lt. Tung left with them to supposedly meet the officer in charge. Sensing danger, Lt. Tung told John to turn back. Instead, John refused, saying, "It doesn't make much difference what happens to me, but it is of utmost importance that my country learn now whether these people are friend or foe."[1] John had asked the rest of the men to remain with the handcar. A short time later, they were taken prisoner by the Communists and forced to march out of the village.

After a period of waiting, John and Lt. Tung were forcibly disarmed by the Communist soldiers. When John demanded to know by what right they could disarm an American officer, both he and Lt. Tung were shot in the legs and then speared with bayonets. Their bodies were thrown into an open pit at the edge of the village. By evening, knowing that the Communists had long departed, a woman from the village came to bury the bodies, only to find that Lt. Tung was still alive. After a long hospital stay, he proudly described John Birch's final hours.

Later, Captain John M. Birch was buried with full military honors in a mausoleum in Hsuchow, his body having been exhumed from a farmer's field. Inscribed on a stone was a simple tribute to the missionary who had risked everything for his country:

> Captain John M. Birch
> August 25, 1945
> He Died for the Cause of Righteousness

"For unto whomsoever much is given, of him shall be much required: and to whom men have committed much, of him they will ask more." Such a verse describes John Morrison Birch. He was blessed with a Christian home, keen intellect, physical strength, mechanical ability, and an extraordinary aptitude for languages—all gifts that could have been used to satisfy material dreams. Yet he was driven by a love of God that knew no bounds. After the war he had hoped to serve as a missionary in Tibet, even foregoing marriage to do so.

In early 1945, John penned an essay that he titled "The War Weary Farmer." He gave his life following God's call, but his vision lives on for those who stay behind, who are excused from the front lines and combat zones to enjoy the essence of freedom.

Excerpts from "The War Weary Farmer"
by John M. Birch[2]

I want to own some fields and hills, woodlands and streams I can call my own. I want to spend my strength in making fields green, and the cattle fat, so that I may give sustenance to my loved ones, and aid to those neighbors who suffer misfortune. I do not want a life of monotonous paper-shuffling or of trafficking with money-mad traders.

I only want enough of science to enable fruitful husbandry of the land with simple tools, a time for leisure, and the guarding of my family's health. I do not care to be absorbed in the endless examining of force and space and matter, which I believe can only slowly lead to God.

I do not want a hectic hurrying from place to place on whizzing machines or busy streets. I do not want an elbowing through crowds of impatient strangers who have time neither to think their own thoughts nor to know real friendship. I want to live slowly, to relax with my family before a glowing fireplace, to welcome the visits of my neighbors, to worship God, to enjoy a book, to lie on a shaded grassy bank and watch the clouds sail across the blue.

I want to love a wife who prefers rural peace to urban excitement, one who would rather climb a hilltop to watch a sunset with me than to take a taxi to any Broadway play. I want a woman who is not afraid of bearing children, and who is able to rear them with a love for home and the soil, and the fear of God.

I want of Government only protection against the violence and injustices of evil or selfish men.

I want to reach the sunset of life sound in body and mind, flanked by strong sons and grandsons, enjoying the friendship and respect of neighbors, surrounded by fertile fields and sleek cattle, and retaining my boyhood faith in Him who promised a life to come.

NOTES

Barbour Publishing, Inc., expresses its appreciation to all those who generously gave permission to reprint copyrighted material. Diligent effort has been made to identify, locate, contact, and secure permission to use copyrighted material. If any permissions or acknowledgments have been inadvertently omitted or if such permissions were not received by the time of publication, the publisher would sincerely appreciate receiving complete information so that correct credit can be given in future editions.

Chapter Four
1. James and Marti Hefley, *The Secret File on John Birch* (Garland, Tex.: Hannibal Books, 1995), 81. Reprinted by permission.
2. Ibid., 83–84.
3. Robert H. W. Welch, Jr., *The Life of John Birch* (Boston: Western Islands, 1960), 11–12.

Chapter Five
1. Welch, 14.

Chapter Six
1. Welch, 16–17.
2. Hefley, 135.
3. Ibid., 151.
4. Ibid., 171.

Chapter Seven
1. Welch, 65.
2. Ibid., 129.

SUGGESTED READING

Hefley, James, and Marti Hefley, *By Their Blood: Christian Martyrs of the 20th Century*. Milford, Mich.: Mott, 1979.

_____, *The Secret File on John Birch*. Garland, Tex.: Hannibal Books, 1995.

Tucker, Ruth A., *From Jerusalem to Irian Jaya: A Biographical History of Christian Missions*. Grand Rapids, Mich.: Zondervan, 1983.

Welch, Robert H. W., Jr., *The Life of John Birch*. Boston: Western Islands, 1960.

BETTY OLSEN

ONE

Chicago—1962

She couldn't write a scene as depressing as her life at this moment.

The setting was an old church basement hallway at night, dimly lit, in the middle of a Chicago winter. The walls were gray cement block; the floor, linoleum squares. Upstairs the voices of the faithful could be heard, those who had come for the midweek prayer service. The service had just ended, and people were milling about before putting on heavy winter coats, scarves, and gloves. In a basement room a few feet away, she could distinguish two voices, one teenaged and one older, though not speaking at the same time. The tired-looking clock on the wall, retired from some parishioner's kitchen, read a minute before eight.

She was twenty-eight years old and unmarried. That was how she thought of herself, period. Although she had a decent job as a nurse, she had few close friends and no—as in zero—prospects among the opposite sex. She was tired of people telling her she was cute, perky, or even attractive. Why say things like that when men don't feel the same way? And if one more person made a comment about her reddish auburn hair—as if that were her only redeeming feature! She wanted to tell the world that having that color of hair was obviously a handicap in her case.

She slid her back up and down the wall to relieve her obvious tension. When the door finally opened a few minutes later, she jumped. A boy about seventeen with a pimply face hurriedly walked past, trying not to make eye contact. She barely looked at him, either. Clearing her throat, she walked the few feet and knocked on the open door.

"Hi," said a man a few years younger than she. He was seated on a Sunday school classroom chair but immediately got up and came toward her. "I'm Bill Gothard."

"My name is Betty Olsen," she said. There was an awkward pause as he ushered her inside with his hand. "I know you talk to young people on Wednesday nights, and I know you don't have an appointment right now. . . ." She looked down at her hands.

"You want to talk now? Sure, have a seat. That's what I'm here for."

Slowly and gently, Bill started asking her questions about herself. Self-conscious at first, she began by offering only the barest details. As he continued probing, though, she started to feel better. No one had seemed that interested in her for a long time. She realized that he was only doing this because she had showed up in this dingy basement room when nobody else was around. Still, it felt good to talk.

Finally, Bill said, "Betty, I can tell you have some problems. But before we start to work on them, I have one question for you. Do you want God's best for your life? If you don't, it won't matter what we do together. You have to be able to say yes honestly."

"What does that mean, 'God's best'? I've been a Christian

since I was a little girl. I try to want what God wants, but then other things get in the way. Maybe I shouldn't be here after all. I mean, you really don't know what you're dealing with here."

"Betty, I want to help you. Please hear me out. Wanting God's best means accepting the way God made you and feeling satisfied by His creation. He did His best. Now you have to work on the inside until you have made your life the best for God."

She might have laughed if she heard those words from some people, but Bill looked so sincere and thoughtful, and he was certainly easy to talk to. She had heard he had had success with the youth group at the church—for what that mattered. Her eyes filling with tears, she wouldn't wish any young person to have her problems or her life. Then the tears spilled over and ran down her cheeks, under her glasses, and off her chin. Before she could find a tissue in her purse, Bill had a box handy.

Finally, she said, "I just want to be happy. What I really want is to be a happy Christian. Does that make sense? Does that answer your question?"

Bill opened his Bible and began to read. " 'For you created my inmost being; you knit me together in my mother's womb. I praise you because I am fearfully and wonderfully made; your works are wonderful, I know that full well'— Psalm 139, verses 13 and 14. Betty, you are exactly the way God wanted you to be, and He loves you just like that."

Betty looked up at him, her eyes red but dry. God's Word could still penetrate her bitter resolve, despite her best efforts to the contrary. When was the last time she had felt that she was wonderfully made? When was the last time she felt God's love? She usually equated the presence of God with the warmth and nearness of a family, not to mention a husband

and children of one's own. In her heart, though, she knew one couldn't put such restrictions on an omnipotent God.

Bill continued to read from the Bible and then wrote down some verses for Betty to look up on her own. When Betty read these verses, she was to think of herself and how she fit into God's plan.

Their "session" finished, Betty and Bill made arrangements to meet again the next week. After putting on a snug woolen stocking cap and bulky car coat, and then cramming her long, thin fingers into gloves, Betty headed out into the frigid air. She needed time to walk and think. Much as she hated to do this, she needed time to remember. But there were so many lost years.

TWO

The last "happy" birthday she celebrated with her family was when she turned eight years old. When she blew out the candles on her cake, she had closed her eyes and forgotten to make a wish. What was there to wish for? Everything seemed just right.

She had been born in the Ivory Coast, or the Cote d'Ivoire, to sound like a native, in the city of Bouake. Bouake, a major metropolitan center, was not on the coast, but inland, not too far from the mountains. Still, the weather was usually hot and humid in this West African country, ideal for playing outdoors. Her parents were missionaries based in Bouake, but her father's job as a church planter and evangelist frequently took him and her mother away from the station. Often Betty and her younger sister, Marilyn, would go along, too, especially when they visited other African churches. They liked to hear the sounds of different languages and be part of the exuberant worship services.

Because the Ivory Coast was a French colony, French was spoken throughout the country, but it was not the dominant language. Many ethnic groups from other African countries had immigrated to the Ivory Coast, and a variety of dialects could be heard, especially in a city like Bouake. Besides his other responsibilities, Walter Olsen was working on translating the book of Matthew into the Baoulé language.

Betty could still see all the happy faces at her birthday party. Of course, Marilyn, who was three years younger, was there, but so were all her African friends. Her father was there, too, laughing and smiling. Everyone liked to be around the tall and gentle man from America. People said Betty looked like him, but her most noticeable feature, her auburn hair, she had gotten from her mother. Mother was racing around, working too hard, making sure everyone had something to eat. Whenever she passed Betty, she gave her daughter a hug and sometimes a kiss on top of her head. *Mama must really love me,* Betty remembered thinking.

That night, Betty couldn't sleep. The wall between her room and her parents' wasn't that thick, and she began to hear voices talking in low tones. She concentrated as hard as she could on what they were saying. "We'll tell them in a few days," her father said.

"Do we have to do it that soon?" her mother asked.

"The sooner, the better. It won't get any easier."

Now Betty really couldn't sleep. The "them" her father was referring to had to be Marilyn and her. She would try to talk to her mother tomorrow—after her father went out about his business. Or maybe she would just wait. Maybe her father would be too busy to tell "them."

The next day, Betty climbed up her favorite tree in the yard and sat there staring out at nothing in particular. She had brought her latest Cherry Ames book to read—about nurses, what else?—but she was too preoccupied to think about anything but her father's ominous words the night before. Suddenly, looking down, she realized she wasn't alone. Marilyn was standing on the ground, hugging the trunk. Her sister spent most of her time outside, so Betty wasn't surprised to see her there.

"Have you seen Daddy?" Betty said in greeting, her mind still mired on one track.

"Yup, he's inside, but he's leaving soon," Marilyn said.

At that, Betty nimbly climbed down. She could trust Marilyn's information, and there was no time like the present to assuage her raging thoughts. Running inside the big old house with its raftered high ceilings, she yelled for her father, her voice bouncing off the walls.

"Daddy, what were you saying last night to Mother? You said you'd tell us in a few days, but I want to know *now*."

Walter Olsen shook his head at his daughter. She always assumed he would know what she was talking about, as if they were in the middle of a conversation. This time, though, he did know, and he knew the subject couldn't be put off indefinitely. Betty, with her hands on her hips and her foot tapping the floor, wouldn't let him rest until she was satisfied with his answer.

"Please tell Marilyn to come inside for a moment and then we'll talk about this together," Walter said calmly. He sat down while Betty followed his order without her usual comments. When the girls returned, he continued. "For the last few years you've both been schooled by your mother here at home, whenever she had time. But your mother and I have known for a while that you aren't receiving a proper education. Now that Betty has turned eight and Marilyn five, well, now is the time to go to a real school with real teachers."

Betty and Marilyn looked at each other and nodded at

their father. Their mother was in the living room, too, leaning against a doorway. Her eyes were sad, Betty thought.

"There isn't a school in Bouake that is suitable for the children of missionaries," Walter said softly.

"Do we get to ride on a bus?" Marilyn asked eagerly, her eyes lighting up at the thought.

"A train and a bus, my dears. Your mother and I have decided that you must go to the missionary school in Guinea, a distance from here. We will see you as often as we can and on all the school holidays. But the school will have to be your home for several months during the year."

Betty felt her throat close up so she couldn't talk or even breathe. Then the tears came, streams of them that coursed down her rosy cheeks. She knew only one thing to do, and that she did. She ran to the open arms of her mother who enveloped her in a hug. Stroking her hair, her mother was saying all the same things her father had, in her wonderful voice, words that sounded foreign to the eight-year-old girl. Following her sister's lead, Marilyn soon joined them—and then her father came over, too.

But that was too much for Betty. How could her parents, who said they loved her so much, do this to her? Pushing her father aside, Betty ran out of the house and back to the safety of her tree. They couldn't make her leave her home. They couldn't do anything to her that she didn't want.

But they could and they did. From the time she was eight until she was in her teens, Betty attended a school for the children of missionaries in Mamou, Guinea, in French West Africa, eight months of the year. Mamou was more than five hundred miles from Bouake, and with each mile, Betty missed her parents all the more. Unlike many children at the school who had embraced new friends and sought new adventures, Betty mostly longed for her family and home. When she and Marilyn did return home for four months—a vacation divided between Christmas and the summer holidays—Betty wasn't overjoyed to be there, either. She wanted to be happy with her family, but she couldn't warm up to them right away when she knew she'd be leaving soon anyway.

When she was almost fourteen, her mother, Elizabeth, who was also called Betty, was diagnosed with cancer. Betty had just begun her freshman year in high school, but not in Mamou. Instead, her parents had decided that she would attend the Hampden DuBose Academy in Zellwood, Florida, an international Christian boarding school for boys and girls. Now she was farther away from home than ever before, and at a time when her mother needed her most.

Betty endured life at the academy. On the surface, the school, which was built on a millionaire's estate, seemed too good to be true, with beautiful grounds and stylish, Spanish-style buildings. Persian rugs and crystal chandeliers graced many of the interiors, while palm trees and flowering azalea bushes painted the landscape. Betty, though, could sum up her existence there in one word: rules. All students were required to do jobs around the school, jobs that had to be done on time and efficiently. All too often, Betty found herself cleaning bathrooms or doing kitchen duty. Finding herself on the outside since her schooling in Mamou, Betty fashioned herself a rebel. She was not going to obey every rule to the letter!

Even though Hampden DuBose was a Christian school, Betty felt, as the child of missionaries, that she was at the bottom of the social pecking order. Her classmates were children of famous evangelists and pastors. She couldn't claim a famous lineage or congregation, and she was too unsure of herself to forge a new path in a strange environment.

After two years Betty was "rescued" from the academy, though not in the way she would have wanted. When her mother's cancer reappeared, Walter made the decision to move the family back to Nyack, New York, with a detour for a year in California. During Betty's freshman year in Florida, Elizabeth had returned to the United States for an operation and then, after a time, went back to Bouake. Now she wanted her entire family with her as she pursued another cancer treatment. Betty left the academy, happily proclaiming that she would have run away if Walter hadn't come for her. Walter heard what she said, but he had other things on his mind.

A few weeks before Betty's seventeenth birthday, in 1951, Elizabeth Kennedy Olsen died. Betty's faith had wavered since her early childhood days in the Ivory Coast, but she had never stopped believing in God. When her mother first became ill, Betty knew there was only one answer to her mother's condition: God would hear her prayers and heal her. God couldn't help but listen to the earnest and lengthy prayers of a daughter who had been forced to live away from her family. But not only had Betty's family ceased to listen to her concerns, to the flame-haired teenager, God had done likewise.

At almost seventeen, Betty was without a mother, permanent home, and friends, not having lived in any place long enough to forge lasting relationships. As if her eighth birthday party were yesterday, she remembered the hugs and kisses on her head, and she also vividly recalled the sadness in her mother's eyes one day later. Her mother had known what it was like to say good-bye. Betty didn't think she could ever master that lesson.

Elizabeth's death had left Walter Olsen in a terrible quandary, too. Not only had he lost his partner of almost twenty years, he was without a job in the United States and money was running out. The Christian and Missionary Alliance (C&MA), which had sponsored him in Bouake, was urging him to return to the mission field. He had been one of the first C&MA missionaries to serve in the Ivory Coast, and Bouake had become the first established C&MA mission station. While he had served previously as a pastor in Poughkeepsie, New York, his heart was with the people of French West Africa, and he felt God was calling him there.

Once he had decided to return to Bouake, Walter faced one of the most agonizing decisions of his life. Would he send Betty back to the academy in Florida? And what would he do with Marilyn, who was about to begin her freshman year in high school? Betty's feelings about being sent away to school were painfully well known. His oldest daughter knew how to speak her mind, he thought with a strong sense of admiration.

An orphan himself since the age of six, Walter was torn between his desire to have his daughters with him or hundreds or thousands of miles away in a formal school. Throughout his own childhood, which had been spent being shuffled from one relative to another, he had never felt truly loved. Now he was sending his own daughters away again, after they had suffered an incalculable loss. He had only one recourse. He would trust God to take care of them. That was the only solution for a single missionary parent.

His mind made up, Betty and Marilyn were both enrolled at Hampden DuBose Academy. Marilyn had always had an easier time adjusting to boarding school, and Walter knew that she would make friends. As for Betty, this would be her senior year. She would just have to make the best of the situation, knowing that she would leave the following year.

Upon graduation, Betty decided to enter nursing school. Those blissful days spent high up in "her" tree in Bouake, a Cherry Ames novel propped up on her knees, were some of her most cherished memories. When her father's sister, Aunt Leona, encouraged her to come to Brooklyn, New York, Betty found a nursing school there, at New York Methodist Hospital. She would live at the school but visit her aunt and other relatives whenever she could. Walter, after all, was not due to be home on furlough for at least two years. Her eyes lighting up at the possibilities of life in a big city among all those doctors, Betty looked forward with a desperate eagerness to the next stage of her life. At last she was about to live out her destiny!

THREE

Betty dusted off the graduation photo and put it on the table beside her bed. If she really looked like a nurse, that's because she was one, she thought. All the graduates were required to pose with their starched white caps pinned neatly in place on the backs of their heads. In the photo she was leaning forward on her elbows, her hands clasped together, her gaze directed outward as if dreaming of some lofty goal. Her training completed, she was about to live the life she had only dreamed about while perched in her tree in Bouake.

Well, not quite. She had been brought down to earth after making countless beds and changing just as many bedpans. And not all nurses were as sheltered as she or claimed nursing as a higher calling. In nursing school she had once again felt like an oddity, though she had made more friends than she had before.

As a registered nurse, she was promptly hired by the New York Hospital to be in the maternity ward, taking care of all those newborns. In 1950, the five thousandth baby had been born at the hospital. Judging from the number she saw under her care, Betty could tell that the predicted "baby boom" was for real. Of course, news of her position had been relayed to Bouake, and congratulations came back from her father and new stepmother.

Shortly after Betty's high school graduation in 1953, Walter had married Gene Sperling, another missionary. They were due to come home on furlough in 1956, and Betty looked forward to meeting Gene then, or so she tried to tell herself. She still missed her mother and, deep inside, she couldn't deny her lingering feelings that her father had deserted her in high school. Those feelings, though, could be filed away for now. She was simply too busy to deal with them.

Since 1881 New York Hospital had been situated in the Park Slope section of Brooklyn, home to many ethnic groups. Betty loved holding all the babies in her care, especially the dark-haired Italian ones. Her father's side of the family was mostly Norwegian, and her mother had been Irish, so these little faces were a welcome change. In no time, maternal feelings began to well up inside her, and Betty began to think seriously about being a wife and mother. To make ends meet, she also began baby-sitting for some of the doctors and learning how to cook at the same time. With a budding reputation as a gourmet chef specializing in Italian dishes, it wasn't long before she began entertaining, too.

For the first time in her life, Betty had met men who wanted to take her out on dates. Regarding those men, Betty thought she didn't really like any well enough to marry and they didn't like her that much, either. Still, it was fun to be wanted.

Betty now had a career, a temporary home, and friends

and even family nearby. Yet, to her, things weren't right. *Why do I always think I'm a missionary?* she woke up debating many mornings. *Is God telling me that's what I should be doing?* Shaking her head, she would then list mentally all the reasons why she would make the worst missionary, beginning with her rebellious and obstinate personality. In the opposite column of her list, being a nurse would definitely be a plus on the mission field—but she lacked missionary training. She thought of her capable father, who had earned the respect of so many. He had even been promoted to chairman of the Ivory Coast mission field.

After she had written her father about her concerns, he wrote back that perhaps she would like to join her sister as a student at Nyack College in Nyack, New York. Walter had met Betty's mother there as a student almost thirty years earlier, and Marilyn had enrolled promptly upon graduation from high school. Betty could even live in Nyack with Walter and Gene when they returned the following summer. Nyack College, under the auspices of the Christian and Missionary Alliance, was a well-known training ground for missionaries. Having lived in Nyack during the traumatic time before her mother's death, Betty could visualize the picturesque campus perched on the banks of the Hudson River. She decided to apply as a missions major, though she was still unsure about her call to the field.

Striking out as she was with the men in Brooklyn, she jokingly told herself, this move just might be the answer to prayer. *Maybe at Nyack I'll meet the man of my dreams*, she thought. *God wouldn't lead me to the mission field without a husband!*

In 1956 Betty was twenty-two years old and about to start college for the first time. But before she crossed that hurdle, she had to meet her new stepmother. As she watched Walter and Gene coming toward her off the ship docked in Manhattan's harbor, she was taken aback at first. She had known Gene was expecting a child, but she didn't expect the sight of her swollen body to come as such a shock. Betty, who wanted desperately to get married and have a child, was face-to-face with the woman about to bear her own sister or brother. Her eyes stung with tears when she looked into the face of her father. Walter seemed happier than she could remember him. Yes, he had smothered her with hugs and kisses and told her how much he had missed her. But all Betty chose to recall was how he looked at the radiant Gene. It was the same way he had once looked at Elizabeth.

The homecoming scene was everything Betty had dreaded, and more. But things were about to get worse. Betty knew she couldn't keep her mouth shut for long.

A few nights later at dinner, Walter started talking about another missionary couple in the Ivory Coast whom Betty didn't know. "They're expecting their first child soon, and of course we couldn't be happier," he said, in reference to his own child to come.

Betty, toying with her food, said nothing—at first. Since meeting Gene at the pier in New York, Betty had been able to block out her pregnancy, and now it was the furthest thing from her mind. Then, without warning, she dropped her fork to the plate. "How could you be so happy?" she cried loudly. "Why any missionary would want to have a child is beyond me! In a few years they just have to send them away, and then the poor children suffer. I can't believe you would say that!"

"Betty, please—" Walter's words were cut off as Betty promptly left the table and marched out of the house.

Betty would live with Walter and Gene for the entire year, a tension-filled time that would be punctuated by similar outbursts. Life was easier once Betty started college. She had decided to attend school part-time and work part-time as a nurse at nearby Nyack Hospital. When Gene had her baby at the hospital, Betty was in the delivery room with her, happy to be there to welcome her new brother. When the year was over and Walter, Gene, and the baby had to return to Africa, Betty was sad to see them go.

Betty had good memories of Africa, especially her growing-up years in the Ivory Coast. She promised Walter and Gene she would come for a visit. To herself she thought, *When I graduate from college would be a good time—and maybe I'll surprise them by staying on as a missionary.*

FOUR

Chicago, 1963

The church basement that had once looked depressing to Betty all those months ago now beckoned her warmly. She had to admit that she looked forward to Wednesday nights, and that the youth group counselor hadn't disappointed her. It had been a year since she first met Bill Gothard, and in that time she had become a different woman.

Betty Olsen the rebel was still alive and well, but the negative, bitter feelings of self-loathing had been replaced by positive, life-affirming thoughts that she was made and loved by a wonderful heavenly Father. Moreover, Betty Olsen the "old maid" had been replaced by a single woman who was proud and happy to serve God in that capacity. Betty had come to accept that she would not marry and to look forward to where God was leading her to serve. Recently, she had applied to be a missionary with the C&MA, with her first choice being Africa. She was waiting to hear from them.

As she watched her boots make neat imprints in the snow, Betty's thoughts drifted back to 1961, when she visited her parents in the Ivory Coast. She was still single, still angry, and still somehow determined to become a missionary with her newly minted missions degree from Nyack College. She was twenty-seven years old and feeling more like a sorry spinster every day. This trip back "home" would remind her of happier days, she thought.

She should have known things were going to be bad when the airline lost her luggage and she didn't get her bags back until almost two months later—when she was about to come home! Betty laughed out loud, her breath forming frosty circles that rose gracefully in the night air. Instead of showing that she had the heart of a missionary, Betty had spent most of her time catching up with African friends from childhood. After arriving home late one night on the back of a friend's motorcycle, Betty was told by another missionary at the station that perhaps it would be best if she went back to the United States. To Betty, the situation had become familiar. The Ivory Coast was another place governed by rules she couldn't abide by. Definitely time to go home, wherever that was.

While Marilyn had settled in Philadelphia, Betty was drawn to Chicago, quickly finding another nursing job, a basement apartment, and a new church home. How God had led her willful feet here, she did not know. She could only praise Him every day.

Bill had directed her to several verses he called "personal disciplines of love." On a piece of paper folded inside her Bible, she had listed these carefully:[1]

Romans 14:7; 1 Corinthians 8, 10: "Don't live to myself."

Ephesians 5:16: "I will make the best use of my time."

> Matthew 18:15; Matthew 5:24: "I will follow
> Scripture when disharmony arises."
> 1 Peter 2:23: "I will expect many opportunities to
> be accused falsely."
> Romans 13: "I will cheerfully accept every respon-
> sibility as from the Lord."
> Hebrews 10:24: "I will seek to build God's Word in
> the lives of others."

As Betty knocked on the door of the basement classroom, she was glad to be there, but another feeling was
clamoring for attention in her soul. God was calling her,
at last, to the mission field. She had accepted herself for
who she was, and she was now ready to make a significant
contribution to the body of Christ. She was ready to go to
the ends of the earth.

In the waning months of 1963, Betty received word from the
C&MA that she was accepted as a missionary. However, there
were already enough missionaries in Africa at the time. Would
she be willing to go to Vietnam as a missionary nurse? Betty
committed the matter to prayer, asking for support from Bill
Gothard and members of her church. While awaiting God's
direction, she plunged herself into study about the war-torn
Indo-Chinese country that had recently been in the news.
What she found was a long history of conflict that presented
no simple resolution.

Since the early 1500s Vietnam had been coveted by
European countries for its natural supply of spices, especially
pepper. While Portugal was the first to establish a permanent
settlement, other European countries followed, only to be
rebuffed by the Vietnamese people time and time again.
Foreigners were not welcome in Vietnam—at least not until

the seventeenth century, when the first Catholic missionaries arrived. Thousands of Vietnamese were converted to Christianity, and trade between Europe and Vietnam began, at last, to flourish. Of special note was the French Jesuit priest Alexandre de Rhodes, who arrived in Vietnam in 1627. He became the first to transcribe the Vietnamese language into characters of the Roman alphabet, which then opened the door for the first translation of the Bible into Vietnamese. Before he died in 1660, de Rhodes claimed to have baptized almost seven thousand Vietnamese.

With the arrival of French missionaries, France itself entered the fray that would decide which European country would claim Vietnam as its colony. After a successful campaign, France emerged the victor, governing Vietnam from the 1880s until World War II. When Japan invaded Vietnam in 1940, a resistance group of Vietnamese nationalists known as the Viet Minh emerged under the leadership of Ho Chi Minh. While the Viet Minh helped the United States war effort, their primary focus was to wrest control of their country from the French.

Following World War II, after a series of skirmishes, the French suffered a major defeat at Diem Bien Phu and decided to leave Vietnam. They had been aided in their battles by the United States, but the cost of continuing the conflict was too great. In 1954, at a meeting in Geneva, Switzerland, a series of agreements was drawn up that plotted out French withdrawal from Vietnam and the future of the troubled country. The Geneva accords divided Vietnam at the 17th parallel, with Ho Chi Minh's Viet Minh forces confined to the north of the country and Emperor Bao Dai in control of South Vietnam.

Soon, however, South Vietnam was in danger of collapsing, due in part to a repressive new government that had been sanctioned by the United States and elected into power in the mid-1950s. The time was right for the Viet Minh, now dubbed "Viet Cong," a slur in reference to their Communist sympathies, to reenter the south. American presence in South Vietnam increased in late 1963 following a coup in the government, the assassination of John F. Kennedy, and the instability of several successive governments. To justify such action to the American public, the term *domino theory* was coined: If one country, such as Vietnam, succumbed to the Communists, that might lead to the Communist takeover of all of Southeast Asia. After the United States was (supposedly) fired upon by the North Vietnamese in the Gulf of Tonkin in mid-1964, the first air strikes against Ho Chi Minh's government were carried out. Support from the United States Congress came overwhelmingly in the form of the Gulf of Tonkin Resolution, which gave "war-making powers" to President Lyndon B. Johnson until "peace and security" had returned to Vietnam.

For American missionaries in Vietnam in the early 1960s, the increased military presence of the United States spelled extreme danger. To the Viet Cong, any and all Americans were imperialists who wanted to control Vietnam much like the French had done. Betty was well aware that in May of 1962 three missionaries had been taken at gunpoint by Viet Cong from a leprosy hospital near Banmethuot, in the central highlands of South Vietnam. Archie Mitchell, the director of the hospital, Dr. Ardel Vietti, a medical doctor, and Dan Gerber, a Mennonite missionary, had not been heard from since their capture, despite the best efforts of the C&MA and the United States government. Like many others, the three hospital workers had presumed they were safe because they were helping native tribespeople—but no American missionary was safe anymore.

Soon Betty became convinced that God was indeed leading her to serve in the troubled country of Vietnam. After garnering sufficient financial support, Betty prepared to leave. She would be joining the largest C&MA presence ever assembled there, a presence that had been at work in the field since 1911. First, though, she would settle in Hong Kong for orientation, and then she would head for Danang, on the northern coast of South Vietnam, for language studies. But all too soon her fate would be bound to one place, along with nine other missionaries. Betty Olsen would find herself at Banmethuot.

FIVE

Banmethuot, South Vietnam——1965

Betty looked out the window of the small plane at the dense vegetation below. *There's nothing but jungle down there*, she thought, trying to summon her normally brave outlook. A few days earlier in Danang she had been interviewed by a columnist for an American newspaper syndicate who had asked her if she felt uneasy being in a war zone. She had replied truthfully, "God called me to be a missionary. I have no fear because I am in the center of God's will."

Now, she had to admit, that resolve was shaking a bit. As the crude runway near Banmethuot came into view, she realized that she was as nervous about meeting the other missionaries as being surrounded by a hostile jungle. Would they accept her as one of them? Or would she have to prove herself over and over again? They certainly wouldn't be threatened by how she looked, she assured herself with a laugh.

She found a mirror in her purse and gave herself a once-over. She now wore her hair shorter than in her Brooklyn nursing days, with her auburn locks shaped like a cap around her makeup-free face. Her bangs were cut as usual, a small fringe an inch or so above her eyebrows. Much to her surprise, she had been quite popular among the American GIs in Danang, with several asking her out on dates. Asserting her new self-image, she had turned them all down.

On the ride to the compound, Betty got the grand tour from a friendly GI who was stationed at the U.S. 155th helicopter base four miles from the missionaries.

"We're on what's called Highway 14," he announced. "That takes you right through Banmethuot to the missionary compound, and it keeps going to the headquarters of Darlac Province officials. That's why it's of interest to the Viet Cong."

The jeep slowed as they entered the provincial capital of Banmethuot. Although the city of thirty thousand appeared rundown and even squalid, Betty had read that it was considered very important to the Viet Cong. "Thousands of tribespeople come to Banmethuot to do their business," the GI explained in answer to Betty's query. "Right next to the mission there's a Raday church, and I'm sure Mnongs come to the clinic there, too," he said, naming the two most common tribes of the area. "You'll get to know them well."

Betty couldn't help noticing that despite the poverty of the city, the surrounding countryside was marked by, at times, outrageous beauty. Indeed, the decrepit movie theaters of the town with their peeling paint were in stark contrast to the peaceful farmland and waterfalls that could be found a few miles away. In Banmethuot she spied desperately poor children smoking cigarettes and, a few miles later, water buffalo, emerging from mudholes in the wild.

"Here we are," the GI said as they came to a stop in front of the compound. "I'm sure we'll see each other again. Stay safe, okay?"

Grabbing her suitcases, Betty mumbled her thanks. After walking a few steps, she put her bags down and gazed around her. Inside the compound were three Italian villa-style residences, as well as other small houses behind them, that she guessed were home to some of the missionaries. She was about to go knock on a door when she heard a voice behind her.

"You must be the new nurse." The woman, who was about Betty's age, was smiling pleasantly. "I'm Ruth Wilting."

"Betty Olsen," Betty said quickly, offering her hand. "You were expecting me?"

"Well, yes, though I was kind of hoping they would send a man to help out when some of the others go on furlough."

"I'm pretty handy," Betty said with a nervous laugh.

"Good. Listen, I didn't mean to imply anything. I'm sure you'll be great, and we can always use another pair of hands, especially at the clinic. Come on, I'll show you to our rooms. We live across the highway with another nurse, Millie Ade."

It didn't take long for Betty to get her bearings within the cozy compound. On one side of Highway 14 were the Raday church, the clinic, and the villas and houses where Betty Mitchell, Carolyn Griswold, and Bob and Marie Ziemer lived. Across the street was the nurses' residence and the Raday Bible School, as well as a South Vietnamese Army base that guarded the southern approach to the city of Banmethuot. The leprosy hospital where the kidnapped missionaries had worked was twelve miles away, in an area thought to be unsafe for American missionaries. Since 1962, Christian Raday nurses operated the "leprosarium" there, coming frequently to the clinic in Banmethuot for supplies.

Following Ruth's lead, Betty also learned what was

expected of her at the clinic. She was an extremely skilled nurse, but she had never worked as a missionary. What she really wanted to do was to work with the young people in the area. Bill Gothard had opened a door for her, and now she felt she could serve a similar role in Vietnam. Until she felt more comfortable speaking the language, though, she simply followed Ruth's direction. Betty especially enjoyed when they made trips outside the compound to villages considered both safe and questionable.

In 1966, both the Ziemers and Ruth Wilting left on furlough for the United States, where they would spend the next year. Ruth, who had been the fiancée of Dan Gerber, one of the three abducted missionaries, was anxious to go home and spend time with her family. She had been sewing her wedding dress when Dan was taken. The dress had been carefully put away, but her feelings were very much on the surface. On her furlough Ruth also intended to meet Dan's family in Ohio for the first time. Betty Mitchell, whose husband, Archie, was also kidnapped, remained stoically at Banmethuot, waiting for news of his whereabouts. During that same year, Carolyn Griswold's mother died, and when she returned from a visit to the United States, her father, Leon, followed her back to the compound. Now that he was alone, he felt he might be of some help to his daughter and the other missionaries.

By the middle of 1967, the missionaries residing at Banmethuot were a different group than when Betty had first arrived. Living in the villas were Bob and Marie Ziemer, who had returned from Ohio; Carolyn Griswold and her father, Leon; and Ed and Ruth Thompson, who had been serving in Cambodia since 1948 and were now temporarily living in Banmethuot until their new home in Quang Duc was completed. Ed spoke a Mnong dialect but was eager to learn the Vietnamese language while at the mission compound. (Betty Mitchell and her family had gone back to the United States on furlough, vacating another house behind the villas.) Living with Betty in the house across the highway were Ruth Wilting and Olive Kingsbury, who had moved in when Millie Ade left on furlough. Three blocks from the compound, Wycliffe Bible translator Hank Blood had moved into a house with his wife, Vange, and their three children. Hank, who had been working on a Bible in the Mnong dialect, was forced to leave a tribal village forty miles away due to great numbers of Viet Cong in the area.

At Banmethuot, as the year drew to a close, the Viet Cong were becoming increasingly active. In early November, Betty could hear the sound of artillery fire at night, the pounding shaking the walls of her house. By the middle of the month, word was out that the Viet Cong had boasted they would take Banmethuot before Christmas. Betty, who had never been happier about her work and her life, knew she was where the Lord wanted her. Still, as the other missionaries' children returned to the compound for their Christmas holiday from school—yes, she thought, they, too, had been sent away from home—Betty felt more anxious than usual. While she and Ruth and Olive made sure the clinic was well stocked and ready for an emergency, they also made plans to celebrate the birth of Jesus. The Christmas Eve service was going to be special this year. A new Raday church, which would be dedicated a week later, would be the site of the service.

On Sunday, Christmas Eve, Ed Thompson preached to a packed church of more than a thousand tribespeople and missionaries. At the service a Mnong named Tang, who had been Hank Blood's language teacher, was baptized. In his village, Tang was the only person Hank had been able to witness to who had accepted Jesus Christ as his Savior. The next day, Christmas, the church was again jammed to overflowing as Raday young people presided over the service.

Two nights later, the Communists attacked a Raday settlement a few miles from the compound. For three hours, Betty and the other nurses were distraught as they huddled in their house, praying for the gunfire to stop. The horrors of war became too clear for her the next day at the funerals held for victims. "Even babies were gunned down," Betty whispered to Ruth as they went about their tasks at the clinic. Everyone was talking in quiet tones, in reaction to the jarring sounds of the night before.

But the war was coming closer to the compound almost by the week. On January 3, 1968, in the early morning hours, the Viet Cong attacked the U.S. helicopter base and then assaulted the province chief's home only two blocks from the compound. A week or so later, other nearby villages were attacked, leaving many dead or wounded. Those who survived told the missionaries to leave Banmethuot while they had the chance.

Together the missionaries gathered at the clinic to treat the injuries of the tribespeople. Betty said to Ruth, "We can't leave Banmethuot, can we? The Radays and Mnongs need us here."

"No, we are where God wants us. I firmly believe that we are serving Him here."

In their letters home, the missionaries urged family and friends to pray harder than ever before. Their enemy was not just the Viet Cong, but Satan. Hank Blood had written to his mother, "I have the feeling the Lord is going to do something special."[1]

On January 26, Betty and Ruth waited with Olive for her ride to the airstrip. She was going to the U.S. army hospital at Nha Trang for a checkup and would be gone at least a week. Despite the pressure of recent days, Betty laughed and joked with Olive, making Ruth feel better, too. Betty had that kind of laugh. When Olive finally drove off down Highway 14, the nurses waved at her until her outstretched hand disappeared.

All across South Vietnam, people anxiously awaited the week-long lunar new year celebration known as Tet. Traditionally, all fighting stopped during the celebration, as if an unwritten truce had been agreed to by the warring parties. To proclaim the new "year of the monkey," a year that was supposed to bring success, women prepared huge portions of *banh chung,* a dish of rice cakes that had been covered with pickled onion, pork fat, and fish sauce. To ward off evil spirits, the villagers made sure they had an ample supply of lime powder, which they sprinkled around their houses, and long strings of firecrackers.

Monday night, January 29, 1968, the missionaries at Banmethuot went to bed with the sounds of firecrackers ringing in their ears. The popping noise disturbed Betty and Ruth because it sounded like gunfire. Somehow a truce seemed too good to be true.

Shortly after midnight on January 30, new sounds confirmed the nurses' worst fears. There *was* gunfire, then a giant *boom*! Peering out their front window facing the compound, Betty and Ruth could only gasp. The Griswolds' home had been blown apart. "Can you see Carolyn or Leon anywhere?" Ruth whispered in the darkness.

"No, I can only hope they were given some kind of warning. I pray the Thompsons and Ziemers are all right. Do you see them, Ruth?"

But there were no signs of life in the villas as the hours

passed and daylight beckoned. On the highway in front of the compound, South Vietnamese army tanks could be seen firing at invisible attackers. Suddenly, Betty and Ruth saw Bob and Ed race inside the destroyed Griswold home, bullets whizzing over their heads. The nurses were propelled into action.

"Ruth, we have to make sure Carolyn and Leon are all right," said Betty, her eyes never leaving the compound.

"Let's wait for a lull and make a dash then," Ruth answered firmly.

Running as fast as they could, they made it to the Griswolds' safely. The men had removed a beam that had pinned down Carolyn, and now the nurses could examine her while Bob and Ed went to rescue Leon. As far as Betty could tell, Carolyn had a broken leg and was in a state of shock. Leon, however, had died before the men could free him. Betty knew they had to get Carolyn to a hospital, but the situation outside was too dangerous. Radays who had come to see how they were doing said the compound was surrounded by Viet Cong. The only thing they could do was move Leon's body into a storeroom and take Carolyn to the Ziemers' with them.

As they prepared to leave the Griswolds' home, the missionaries watched in horror as a terrible scene unfolded in front of the compound. Mike Benge, a U.S. AID technician and friend to the missionaries, had just pulled up in his jeep and was coming toward their door. Although Ed waved his arms to signal Mike to leave, the former marine hadn't noticed. Within seconds, Mike was surrounded by Viet Cong. He would be their first prisoner. Soon there would be others.

Wednesday, January 31, found the missionaries still holed up at the Ziemers' house. The Bloods were staying in their house a few blocks away, even though Hank and his son had made a furtive trip to check on everyone at the compound. Despite their situation, Betty and Ruth continued making running trips to the clinic. Carolyn was in desperate need of blood and medicine, and there were also wounded Radays waiting at the clinic. Meanwhile, Bob and Ed had dug a trench where the garbage pit was behind the house, in case they needed somewhere to flee to in a hurry.

That night, the Thompsons' house exploded before their eyes. Knowing the Ziemers' house would be next, the missionaries, carrying Carolyn, headed for the servants' house first, where they put her on a cot, and then to the garbage pit. Bullets streaked above and beside them as they jumped into the pit. When daylight came, Betty and Ruth decided to make another trip to the clinic.

Then Betty got another idea. "I'll try to get a car so we can get out of here. We've got to get Carolyn to a hospital soon or she won't make it."

Ruth wasn't sure about this but didn't feel like arguing with Betty. Besides, she could tell Betty's mind was made up. As Ruth made her way to the clinic, Betty ran to one of their cars and climbed inside. But just as she was about to start the engine, bullets shattered the windshield, narrowly missing her. Viet Cong soldiers surrounded the car and then pulled her out, dragging her down the road to the same small house where they had first taken Mike Benge. Betty Olsen would be their second prisoner.

Ruth Wilting was about to return to the pit when she was stopped in her tracks by another explosion. The Ziemer house had exploded in flames. The courtyard was suddenly filled with Communist soldiers looking for survivors. They were heading for the garbage pit.

Suddenly, Bob Ziemer climbed out and ran toward

the soldiers with his hands up, in an effort to stop the attack. He was brutally gunned down, his body landing over a clothesline.

Running toward the others, Ruth cried out, "I don't know what they want!" She was also gunned down, her body toppling into the crude bunker.

Looking down into the pit, the soldiers then gunned down Ed and Ruth Thompson. Ed had thrown himself on top of his wife to save her, but it was too late. The same torrent of gunfire wounded Marie Ziemer, who immediately clutched her left side in agony. A few minutes later, a soldier ordered her out of the pit and led her to where the others were being held. Along with Betty and Mike, the Viet Cong had captured Pastor Y Ngue of the Raday church and several members of his church.

Meanwhile, the soldiers had burst inside the Bloods' home, wounding Vange and one of their daughters. After binding Hank's hands with telephone wire, the soldiers led the family to the tribal house to join the others held captive. With the new additions, the two-room house had become very crowded. Their discomfort, though, was momentarily forgotten at the sound of a helicopter flying overhead and then the sound of more gunfire.

Afterward, one of the soldiers led Betty, at her request, to the clinic to collect her bag. As they passed Bob Ziemer's body, still hanging over the clothesline, the soldier asked Betty, "Where is his gun?"

True to form, Betty answered, "You fool! Missionaries don't have guns!" She proceeded to move Bob's body to a nearby cot.

At the same time, Vange was ordered to get some things for Hank, including his passport. When she returned, she had only seconds to say good-bye to her husband before the group was led away into the jungle.

It was late on Thursday, February 1, 1968.

The next day, Friday, February 2, Marie and Carolyn were flown to the U.S. army hospital in Nha Trang to receive care. Marie would recover, but Carolyn died a few hours later. Vange and her children caught a later plane to the same hospital. Sometime that morning, news of the attack on the mission station reached C&MA headquarters in New York. Of the ten missionaries at Banmethuot, six were dead and two were captured.

There would be no more news of the captives for three years.

SIX

We must have walked miles already, Betty thought as she trudged along behind Pastor Ngue, their hands tied together by telephone wire. Glancing down at her legs, she could see insects had feasted many times over on her bare skin. If only she had worn pants today! She couldn't believe she was wearing a thin summer dress, the fabric torn in places from brushing against prickly plants on their forced march into the jungle.

"How much farther, Pastor Ngue?" she hissed, hoping he might know their destination.

"Not many miles, Amai Betty," he shot back.

"Silence!" shouted the guard to the pastor in the Raday dialect. "You will not talk to American enemies."

When the soldiers ordered them to stop, Betty could see a U-shaped building in the jungle clearing, a building she had heard about but never seen. They were at the leprosarium. Of the Americans, only Mike Benge had been here before—most recently, in the hours after his capture. There he had witnessed the execution of several Raday tribesmen. Had the Communists brought them here for the same purpose?

He didn't want to convey his anxiety to Hank and Betty, at least not yet. Anyway, Betty was preoccupied with her bag, which had just been returned to her by the soldiers.

"The money's gone, Hank," she whispered. "I went to the clinic to get the three thousand dollars we had in cash, and they've stolen it."

"Maybe they'll let us go now," he said encouragingly.

"At least my Bible is still here," she said, a smile brightening her features.

Pastor Ngue, who had never strayed far from Betty, now left her side to talk to the soldiers. "You've taken their money, now release the missionaries. They have come to Vietnam to help people, not to kill them." Then, pointing to Betty, he said, "I have seen Amai Betty scrape the leprous calluses off the feet of the Vietnamese people. She has only come to Vietnam to serve God."

The soldier spit on the ground. "God? There is no God but Ho Chi Minh. These are agents of the CIA, imperialist enemies of the Vietnamese. And that woman. Why is she here without her husband?"

Betty looked into the soldier's face, her gaze never wavering. "I'm not married," she said, her voice becoming more confident. "But I don't need a husband to serve God."

Her heart pounding, Betty then summoned the courage to ask about the three missionaries taken at gunpoint six years earlier from this very spot.

"I do not know those names," the commanding officer said, walking away.

The march through the jungle continued. By day they walked, stopping only to eat. At night they slept chained together in padlocked bamboo cages. There was little time they weren't bound to each other. A few days later, as they walked unchained across a log bridge, Betty, who was among the last to cross, lost her balance and tumbled down, catching herself on a tree limb. During the fall, her glasses fell into the water, lost forever. Mike ran to her rescue, pulling her out and brushing off her dress. She had no broken bones, but she was shaken up. The soldiers ordered her to continue walking.

Finally, when they were at a point far enough from civilization, the telephone wire was removed for good from their wrists and they were allowed more freedom. Since they weren't moving every day, the missionaries had more time to talk to each other. At first Betty, Hank, and Mike talked about their hunger. After more than three weeks as captives, they felt weak from near starvation. Their meals consisted of thin, watered rice, the edible, starchy roots of manioc, and occasionally some vegetables. But Hank, who had kept up a running commentary as they walked, could not stop talking about the Lord. Both he and Betty were unsure where Mike stood or whether he had accepted Jesus into his heart.

Mike, a compact, athletic man who was the same height as Betty, had grown up on a ranch in eastern Oregon. After graduating from Oregon State, like Hank, he entered the marines and then began working as a U.S. AID technician, helping the tribespeople around Banmethuot find better ways to work their land. Like Hank, he spoke the Raday dialect and was familiar with the landscape of Vietnam.

But on the subject of Christianity, Mike shied away. He hadn't thought much about religion since he was a boy. "Besides, I don't think we should be judging each other," he said to Hank.

Hank and Betty, undeterred, continued to read out loud from Betty's Bible every day, several times a day. "Like Daniel, we've been thrown into the lions' den, Mike. We need God more than ever now—and He's there for us in His Word."

When gunfire was heard close by, the North Vietnamese commander ordered camp broken and they began marching again. Betty was sure she had heard planes overhead, too, but there was no way they could be seen under such dense jungle cover. Mike, who possessed a keen sense of direction, felt they were going west toward the mountains. The planes they had heard were probably landing at Nha Trang.

While they were still hopeful of being rescued, their deteriorating health had become a concern. Hank, a tall, gentle man in his late forties, looked especially frail. A dedicated linguist who spent long hours poring over books, he was not used to such unending physical activity. An ugly boil on his hip caused him to cry out at night, waking the Americans and the guards, who threatened punishment if he did it again. All three had bruised feet and scales on their legs and backs, the result of malnutrition, and all of them had succumbed to dengue fever from walking in mosquito-laden swamps. Their pleas for medicine were ignored.

When Hank's condition worsened, Betty approached the commanding officer. "We are no threat to you; you must realize this by now," she said. "If you had any feeling for your Vietnamese people, you would let us go."

"Why should I listen to a woman who has no husband?" he retorted.

"Because I care about you. And because the God you say doesn't exist loves you."

Pastor Ngue, who had heard Betty crying in pain, as well as the moans of Mike and Hank, decided to take matters into his own hands and find natural remedies for their sores. Boiling plant leaves in water and then applying them to the sores brought relief for a while—until Ngue was apprehended by the guards.

"Amai Betty, I have decided to escape soon," he whispered to her one night. "These soldiers think nothing of killing a poor Raday pastor."

"How would you do it?" Betty asked, sensing a way out for herself, as well.

"I would hide some sticks in the woods, and then when my friends and I escaped, we would beat the guards."

Betty shook her head. "No, Pastor Ngue. You can't hurt these people even though they have been cruel. You must leave without hurting anyone."

When Pastor Ngue remained in the camp for several days afterward, Betty turned her thoughts to keeping up the spirits of Mike and Hank. Lately, she and Hank had noticed a change in Mike. He seemed more serious and thoughtful. Every day, Hank continued to talk about having a relationship with Jesus. Mike was listening, but he was tough, Betty thought. *He's always been so self-reliant—that's the problem.* One day she said to him, "Mike, you can't save yourself even if you're a very good person and do good things. Only Jesus can save a person—if they ask Him to come into their heart."

Then Hank opened Betty's Bible to John 1:12. "But as many as received him, to them gave he power to become the sons of God, even to them that believe on his name."

"Once you accept Him, Mike, you're a child of God," Hank said. "That's real power."

A few weeks later, Pastor Ngue came to Betty again. "I have overheard the guards speaking in the Mnong dialect. They did not think I could understand. They intend to kill me and the other Radays in four days. We must leave soon."

"Can't you take me with you?" Betty pleaded. "I've been feeling stronger lately."

Pastor Ngue looked Betty up and down and sadly shook his head. "No, Amai Betty, you would never be able to make the difficult journey. I will be going through jungles and across raging rivers. I may even come face-to-face with wild animals. But I will tell the United States Army. They will find you; do not worry. Besides, Mike needs you here. He is getting worse by the day."

Betty's eyes filled with tears. Her best chance to leave had just vanished. Turning away from the pastor, she returned to where Mike was lying. In the last few days, he had come down with malaria and was slipping in and out of consciousness. *Yes, Pastor Ngue is right,* Betty thought. *There's no way I could leave Mike now.*

Before she fell asleep that night, Betty heard someone whistling a tune. The melody was "God Be with You till We Meet Again." Pastor Ngue was saying good-bye.

Mike was sick with malaria for over four weeks, Betty estimated. In her bag she had found a tiny calendar, and she used that to estimate what month and day it was. Time seemed to move so slowly. Throughout his illness, Betty had stayed by Mike's side as much as she could. When he was shivering from the chills, she wrapped a lice-ridden blanket around him, a "gift" from one of the guards. When he was burning up, she dipped a cloth in water and placed it on his forehead. Mike's hair had turned white, and for a while, he had gone blind.

There was no medicine available, or none the guards would give her, but Betty would not let Mike die, not on her watch. She fed him tiny portions of food, insisting that he eat something. She read him Scripture when his eyes fluttered open and sang him favorite hymns when he drifted off to sleep. Slowly, Mike began to regain his strength and was able to walk. His health had returned just in time, because they were on the move again. It was now the end of May, Mike estimated, and they had covered what he thought to be two hundred miles.

By July, after enduring the torrential downpours of the rainy season without proper shelter, Betty, Mike, and Hank were feeling terrible. They had endured months of little food and no protein and no clean clothes. Even though Mike had survived malaria, all three were painfully thin, their bones showing through their skin.

Moreover, the rains had brought blood-sucking leeches that clung to Betty's bare legs. She barely had the strength to pull them off. Mike noticed that Betty's cheeks, normally rosy and full, were pale and sunken and that her hair hung down in dirty strands around her face.

Hank was in the worst shape of all three. Because of the rain and the cooler temperatures at night, he had developed pneumonia and was coughing uncontrollably. A raging fever had left him so weak that he couldn't lift his head. Still, he loved to read God's Word and had found solace in one verse from Matthew's gospel: "But I say unto you, Love your enemies, bless them that curse you, do good to them that hate you, and pray for them which despitefully use you, and persecute you" (Matthew 5:44). When he couldn't read, Betty read for him.

Again, Mike and Betty begged the guards for medicine. Again, they were refused. One soldier said, "What is he to us? One less enemy to fight. There is nothing you can do for him anyway."

Hank's final words to his friends were full of love for his family and captors, and would they see how Tang was doing, too? Finally, on July 13 or 14—Betty and Mike couldn't be sure of the date—Hank Blood died and was buried by his North Vietnamese guards. At a brief funeral service, Betty recited the Twenty-third Psalm.

Without Hank with them, Betty and Mike started to talk more to each other. Betty liked that Mike seemed genuinely interested in her life and that he really listened to her. Mike appreciated Betty's struggle to find herself as a missionary and admired her obvious spunk and courage. She was the strongest person he had known, and that was saying something. To each other, they had become brother and sister. They would help each other until other help came. They couldn't think otherwise.

But they were overwhelmed by the same health problems that had beset them for months. Their hair was now gray. They had lost all body hair. Their nails had stopped growing. Their gums were bleeding. They were almost powerless to pull off the blood-sucking leeches. Their legs were so swollen that they could barely lift them. To walk, they had to make a determined effort of putting down one leg and lifting the other. Often they were beaten by the guards who insisted they move faster.

Whenever Mike complained to the guards about the leeches killing Betty, the answer was the same: "And your soldiers are killing us."

Betty found herself thinking more about her family and all the years when she was filled with bitterness and resentment. The last time she saw her father was 1962, when he was on furlough in Seattle and about to return to Africa. He had been so pleased to see the change in his daughter's heart. That was the last time she had seen Marilyn, too. This year, 1968, was to have been her furlough year, and she had already made reservations to fly to the Ivory Coast. Now those would have to wait.

Long ago she had forgiven her father and reaped enormous blessings. It was time to forgive her captors, and it was God's will. Together with Mike, Betty prayed out loud, "Lord, whatever You allow is all right. Forgive our enemies. They don't know what they are doing. They don't know who You are."

The march continued day after day. When they crossed Highway 14 near the Cambodian border, Mike felt more hopeful. Maybe someone would see them. There had to be U.S. troops near here. If only Betty could keep going. . .if only she had something better to eat.

But a dinner was to be her undoing. After a meal of corn, rice, and bamboo shoots, Betty and Mike became violently ill. Mike later discovered that the guards had cooked the bamboo shoots only once, and not twice, which was necessary to rid the stalks of all harmful bacteria. Betty became so weak she was unable to get out of her hammock in the morning. Soon she was powerless to leave her hammock at all. The guards ignored her, saying, as they had with Hank, that there was nothing they could do.

Mike refused to leave her side, though it was painful to look at her shriveled body. *They could have saved her,* he thought angrily. *And yet, they have let this good, strong, wonderful woman die.* A few days before she died, Betty whispered to Mike to tell the guards that she loved them, and God loved them, too. He held her thin hand and cried.

Less than a month before her thirty-fourth birthday, Betty Olsen died. She was buried quickly by her captors.

Shortly after Betty died, Mike Benge was put into a prisoner-of-war camp, along with hundreds of American

GIs. It would be the first of several prison camps Mike would find himself in over the next few years, including almost a year spent in one venue in solitary confinement. But everywhere he went, Mike talked to his fellow inmates about Jesus Christ. Hank and Betty's witness was alive and well in the former marine, who was an inspiration to many.

When Mike was released in the spring of 1973, he was flown to an army base on the Philippines where he met Vange Blood, Hank's widow. She had waited all these years for some definite information about Hank. As best he could, Mike told her what had happened to Hank and also to Betty. He couldn't talk about them without his voice cracking.

After drying her eyes, Vange then began telling Mike what was happening at Banmethuot. But before she could say much, Mike interrupted.

"Pastor Ngue? Did he make it back?"

Vange nodded several times. A few months after his escape, Pastor Ngue showed up at the compound. He was so thin after his journey that his family didn't recognize him at first. "Mike, he tried to get the U.S. Special Forces to find you. But at the time they couldn't send out a team."

Mike swallowed hard, thinking again about Betty and Hank. He was glad to hear, though, that all the buildings that had been destroyed at the compound were rebuilt. There was even a memorial erected to the slain missionaries near the makeshift bunker. At the time, Vange and her children were continuing Hank's work, translating the Bible into the Mnong dialect.

"And what about Tang?" Mike asked suddenly, remembering Hank's dying request.

Vange's face brightened at the mention of his name. "Oh, Tang. If only Hank could see him now! Tang is on fire for the Lord, Mike. Thousands of tribespeople have come to know Jesus because of his testimony."

Hank and Betty were right, thought Mike. *There is real power in being a child of God.*

While at Banmethuot, Betty had sent Marilyn a copy of *Hinds' Feet on High Places* by Hannah Hurnard. She also mentioned the book in a letter to Walter and Gene.

As she told her parents and sister, Betty had been touched deeply by Hurnard's allegorical tale of a crippled woman named Much-Afraid who is directed on a journey to the High Places by the Shepherd. Much-Afraid, whose companions are called Sorrow and Suffering, must put her entire trust in the Shepherd if she is to conquer such foes as Craven Fear, Pride, Resentment, and Bitterness. Along the way, she receives the flowers of Acceptance-with-Joy and Bearing-the-Cost, also known as Forgiveness.

When at last Much-Afraid arrives at the High Places, she is given a new name, Grace and Glory. The Shepherd then asks what she has learned on her journey.

" 'I learned that I must accept with joy all that You allowed to happen to me on the way,' " she says. " 'I learned that I must bear all that others were allowed to do against me and to forgive with no trace of bitterness. . . . I learned that You, my Lord, never regarded me as I actually was. . . . You saw me as I would be when You had done what You promised and had brought me to the High Places.' "

On her life's journey Betty Olsen overcame the bitterness that had sprung from an often lonely childhood and adolescence, the resentment she felt at the loss of her mother, and the craven fear she openly admitted of living her life as a single woman. She had to swallow her pride at not being accepted at first as a missionary. When she found that she had no answers and nowhere to turn, the Good Shepherd was there to lead her. Through reading His Word, she was able to accept with joy the way she was made and then bear the cost of serving Him. In the end, she was able, without regret or bitterness, to forgive those who had caused her to suffer greatly and then to die.

Grace and glory were hers.

NOTES

Barbour Publishing, Inc., expresses its appreciation to all those who generously gave permission to reprint copyrighted material. Diligent effort has been made to identify, locate, contact, and secure permission to use copyrighted material. If any permissions or acknowledgments have been inadvertently omitted or if such permissions were not received by the time of publication, the publisher would sincerely appreciate receiving complete information so that correct credit can be given in future editions.

Chapter Four
1. Betty's list, which is seen in a photograph, was taken from *No Time for Tombstones* by James and Marti Hefley (Wheaton, Ill.: Tyndale House Publishers, Inc., 1974).

Chapter Five
1. James C. Hefley, *By Life or Death* (Grand Rapids, Mich.: Zondervan, 1969), 134.

Chapter Six
1. James C. Hefley and Marti Hefley, *No Time for Tombstones* (Wheaton, Ill.: Tyndale House Publishers, Inc., 1974), 89.

SUGGESTED READING

Hefley, James C., *By Life or by Death*. Grand Rapids, Mich.: Zondervan, 1969.

Hefley, James C., and Marti Hefley, *No Time for Tombstones*. Wheaton, Ill.: Tyndale House Publishers, Inc., 1974.

Hurnard, Hannah, *Hinds' Feet on High Places*. Westwood, N.J.: Barbour and Company, Inc., 1977.

Karnow, Stanley, *Vietnam: A History*. New York: Penguin Books, 1983.

Tucker, Ruth A., *From Jerusalem to Irian Jaya: A Biographical History of Christian Missions*. Grand Rapids, Mich.: Zondervan, 1983.

LOTTIE MOON

ONE

April 1865

Lottie could see for herself that the Yankees were getting close. Climbing on top of an old tree stump, then stretching to beyond her four-foot, ten-inch frame, she saw what looked like wisps of smoke in the direction of Carter's Mill. That was only a few miles away. There wasn't a moment to waste.

But what to do first? Even though Lottie was twenty-four years old and a college graduate, she still deferred to the will of her mother. The war had taken a considerable toll on Anna Maria Moon, but she could think clearly and quickly.

"Lottie, the family jewelry and the silver! Go now, hide it somewhere. You'll know best," Mrs. Moon said before giving other instructions to some of the family's slaves. Despite the upheaval of the war, most of them had chosen to remain at Viewmont, the Moon family's plantation home in Albemarle County, Virginia.

Nodding her head at her mother, Lottie turned on her heel and raced up the grand staircase, passing her slowly descending older sister on the way. Orianna, several months pregnant, was gripping the banister with all her strength. As soon as the baby was born, Orie and her husband would be moving to his home in Alabama. But for now, they were one more concern in an already upside-down household.

"Never mind me, Lottie," Orie said. "I need to catch some air. I can barely breathe upstairs."

"Go and keep Mother company, then," Lottie instructed. "I'll take care of things for now."

"I know, Lottie," Orie said, pausing to pat her sister's arm. "You were always the strong one."

Only a weakened Orianna would say something like that, Lottie thought as she watched her sister navigate the rest of the steps successfully. Then, grabbing her hoop skirts, she threw herself again into her mission. Once in her mother's bedroom, Lottie dumped the contents of her mother's jewelry box into a pillowcase and then, bag flying, ran back downstairs to the formal dining room. Into another pillowcase she dumped the ornate silver pieces, kept shined to polished perfection for generations. She felt as if she were carrying two overflowing pails of water as she lumbered outside, her eyes fixed on the apple orchard.

Right behind her were her sisters Colie and Eddie—Sarah and Edmonia—who knew better than to tell their older sister what to do. Lottie, sensing their presence, stopped for a moment, resting the bags on the ground. "Colie and Eddie, we'll need two shovels. We're going to dig holes in the orchard for these pillowcases and mark the places for later. See the smoke? We've got to hurry!"

Seeing them scurrying ahead gave Lottie the confidence to keep going. This was the closest the Yankees had been to Viewmont in all the years of the War between the States. Just a few days ago, Robert E. Lee, the commander of the Confederate forces, had agreed to the terms of surrender offered by his Union counterpart, Ulysses S. Grant. While Grant had thought that Lee meant to fight to the bitter end, the South's beloved general was loath to see his homeland of Virginia suffer greater desecration and bloodshed. Thus, on April 9, 1865, in the hamlet of Appomattox Court House, Virginia, just forty miles from Lottie Moon's home, the war was declared over. The North was victorious.

Sensing that the spoils of war were theirs, some Union soldiers turned to violence and destruction as they made their way back home. Word had spread from farm to farm to beware of these marauding troops, eager to strip what little remained from the depleted Virginia landscape. Where there had once been comfort, refinement, and elegance were ghostly reminders of the aftermath of war—solitary chimneys, charred beams, and brick stairs leading to nowhere. The blue-clad scavengers would find slim pickings unless they possessed secret information.

Gritting her teeth, her blue eyes flashing, Lottie was determined that Viewmont remain unscathed. Lugging the pillowcases to the orchard, she helped her sisters bury the family treasure in two holes and then carefully concealed their efforts. Since the earth had recently been overturned with spring plantings, no soldier would be suspicious of their particular patches of rich Virginia soil.

"Look at my calluses, Lottie! Isn't this good enough for now?" Eddie whined.

Lottie gave her a stern look and was about to say something when she stopped herself. Eddie was just a girl, after all. The last place she wanted to be was in the middle, or on the losing side, of a war.

"Yes, Eddie, that's fine. Now all we have to remember is where we buried the pillowcases."

The three sisters decided to mark places on nearby trees

to indicate where the treasure lay. No one would know the place but them. *Mother would be pleased,* Lottie thought.

But upon returning to the house, Lottie found her mother pacing back and forth, wringing her hands. "Lottie, do you see any soldiers coming? Is the smoke getting closer?"

"No, Mama, there's no one in sight. Everything's buried. I think we're safe for a while."

"Thank you, dear. Perhaps we could gather everyone inside for prayers. At a time like this, we need to pause and thank our heavenly Father."

Later that evening, Lottie lay awake on her bed with only the sounds of insects buzzing in her ears. Whatever soldiers had been nearby were gone—for now. But that didn't mean her worries had fled, too. There were so many unanswered questions.

"Oh, Papa, what would you do if you were here?" she whispered in the darkness. "Would you ever have imagined our life would be like this—five women practically alone in your house with Yankees camped who knows where and pillowcases of your silver and gold buried in the apple orchard?" A giggle burst through her lips at the thought.

She pulled a favorite quilt tighter around her neck and closed her eyes. She was a little girl again with dark brown braids and a mischievous look on her face. As usual, there were grass stains on her dress and crumbs of leftover treats in her pockets. And the best things in the world were climbing trees and eating Mama's tea cakes.

TWO

Her name, but not her personality, bespoke privilege. Charlotte Digges Moon, the third child of Edward Harris and Anna Maria Barclay Moon, was born December 17, 1840, on a plantation that boasted thousands of acres and hundreds of slaves and stood near a byway known as the Road of the Presidents.

Indeed, both sides of her family had rubbed shoulders with the founding fathers of America. Thomas Barclay, her mother's grandfather, settled in Philadelphia just prior to the American Revolution. A friend of George Washington, Thomas Paine, and Thomas Jefferson, he was appointed by the Continental Congress to establish trade relations with France. On her father's side was Sir Dudley Digges, who once served as a colonial governor of Virginia.

Viewmont, one of eight estates belonging to Anna Maria's stepfather, Captain John Harris, was a wedding gift to Lottie's parents. Located to the west of such estates as Jefferson's Monticello, James Madison's Montpelier, and James Monroe's Ashlawn, the mansion was built by Colonel

Joshua Fry, a colonial architect, between 1744 and 1751. The house, which was set on a hill, was flanked by two great chimneys. Typical of the times, the kitchen was contained in a separate building, as were the living quarters of the slaves—some thirty cabins. In the fields behind the house, tobacco, corn, and wheat were grown, but there were large areas devoted to natural forest, too. From the highway below, a long, winding road with orchards to the left provided striking views of, and access to, the estate.

There was little reason for Lottie to leave Viewmont in her early years. The grounds provided ample space to play, and when she tired of her sisters and brothers, she had only to invite her cousins over, who lived on a neighboring estate. Closest in personality and age to her was her "double" cousin James Moon, so called because he was related to her on both sides of her family. Most days would find Lottie and James romping through the woods with some of their dogs, picking raspberries, or climbing trees in one of the orchards.

On a certain summer day, the two were lying on neighboring branches, their legs dangling lazily. With their eyes gazing earnestly at the Blue Ridge Mountains, Lottie gave a sudden, horrible moan.

"What'd you forget now?" James asked, knowing Lottie all too well.

"Another governess arrives today, and I'm supposed to meet her," she answered dully.

"How many does that make?" James knew his cousins had gone through quite a few already.

"You know I'm not good at numbers," Lottie said, laughing at herself. "Mama just expects too much of them. All I'd like is for them to leave me be so I could read what I want to. But Mama wants us to learn French, literature, mathematics, *and* history! This new one's s'posed to get

Thomas ready for university, whatever that is."

"That's so he can become a doctor," James said with a tinge of awe in his voice. Thomas, who was years older than they were, always seemed to be doing something important. "I even heard Orie wants to be a doctor, too. Who ever heard of a woman doctor?"

Lottie stifled a yawn from her perch. "Who ever heard Lottie Moon was on time? You should be thinking of an answer to that rather than worrying about brainy old Orie. Besides, if I don't leave soon, I'm going to get another lecture from Mama!"

James gave Lottie a suspicious sidelong glance. "You mean, if you don't leave now, there won't be any tea cakes left!" In seconds the two were chasing each other across the green fields, the only way they knew to go home.

Despite the allure of her tea cakes, everyone knew that Anna Maria Moon brooked no arguments about the importance of education. But she was also respected for her uncompromising views on attending church and keeping the Sabbath holy. Since Lottie was a young child, the family had been attending the Scottsville Baptist Church, ten miles from Viewmont. Anna Maria and Edward had been instrumental in building the church, but it was Anna Maria who set the spiritual tone of the household. Much to Lottie's dismay, her mother forbade any cooking on Sunday, forcing Lottie to eat cold biscuits and chicken all day!

To Lottie, the only palatable part of her spiritual education was when her mother read her stories about missionaries. Her favorite was of the three Mrs. Judsons, or the three wives of Adoniram Judson, who served in Burma in the 1820s. Of the three women, Lottie liked hearing most about Adoniram's first wife, Ann Judson. Even though Ann was marrying Adoniram knowing full well his desire to go first to India, as a woman she felt called by God to go, too.

Little did Lottie realize that women would be able to be missionaries without having husbands—and that a member of her very family would be among the first.

In January 1852, with Thomas studying medicine at the University of Pennsylvania and Orianna about to begin her medical studies at the Female Medical College of Pennsylvania, tragedy struck the family. On a business trip to New Orleans, Edward Moon was a passenger on a river boat that caught fire. After hoisting his trunk filled with gold coins overboard and swimming to shore himself, Edward collapsed on the sandy beach, dead. Doctors surmised he had suffered a stroke. He would be buried in the family cemetery at Viewmont.

Anna Maria, who had lost her own father in a drowning accident, was accustomed to dealing with crisis. She had watched her mother raise her family alone for years without the support of a husband, and the lessons had stayed with her. First, she implemented a plan to manage the estate. Then she resumed her role as the supervisor of her next daughter's higher education. Two years later, after enduring more governesses for Lottie, Anna Maria pronounced it was time for her willful daughter to go away to school.

Lottie would begin her formal education at the Virginia Female Seminary, which was renamed Hollins Institute one year later. At the school in Roanoke, she would be tested as never before. Only fourteen years old, Lottie would be studying Latin, French, natural science, arithmetic, algebra, and English composition. She would succeed, but she would do so with a twinkle in her eye.

On April Fools' Day, 1855, Lottie decided it was time

to shake things up at the staid academy. Besides, she was tired of hearing the school bell ring at six every morning, jarring her awake from a perfectly pleasant sleep. There would be one morning when that wouldn't happen, she decided to herself. But she would confide her plan to no one. Knowing the other girls, one of them would be sure to spill the beans.

In the early morning hours, Lottie snuck out of bed and out of the girls' dormitory to the chapel. She climbed up to the rafters and then, using all her skills honed in Viewmont's orchards, crawled along the beams until she reached the bell tower. There, at last, was the object of her tomfoolery. After wrapping blankets and towels securely around the bell clacker to the best of her ability, she departed in haste for her bed. Thankfully, all the girls were still asleep. No one would know what had transpired.

When six o'clock came and went without a dong, Lottie could barely contain herself. It was seven o'clock before the school matrons burst into the girls' dormitory to announce that somehow the bell had failed to ring. That day no one discovered that Lottie had been the culprit. It would be her secret until she decided to share it.

One year later, Lottie proudly stood in line to receive her certificate of graduation from Hollins. For most of the young women of the South, this day would mark the end of their formal education. Most, like Lottie's roommate, Carey Ann Coleman, were making plans to get married, even as soon as that summer. Lottie had introduced Carey Ann to her double cousin James, and the two were to wed in June.

Lottie had no such plans, even though she was known to have a beau or two. She had graduated with top grades from Hollins, and she had a thirst to learn more. During the next year, while she bided her time at Viewmont teaching her younger sisters and helping her mother run the estate, scholarly men were meeting in nearby Charlottesville to establish a university program for women. The school, which would open in the fall of 1857, would be called the Albemarle Female Institute but for all purposes would be an extension of the all-male University of Virginia. Virginia professors would teach all the courses offered at the institute, and the standards for graduation would be the same as at the university.

Charlotte D. Moon was among the entering class. As at Hollins, she proceeded to take the most rigorous course of study offered, with her major designated as modern languages. Even though she was serious about her studies, she hadn't lost her sense of mischief. After a particularly satisfying prank, one of her classmates asked what her middle initial stood for.

"The D is for devil," she answered without skipping a beat. "Don't you think it suits me?" So quickly had she responded that everyone believed her.

Two years later, in 1859, Dr. John A. Broadus, the pastor of the Charlottesville Baptist Church, held a revival. Without Anna Maria there to prod her, Lottie had no intention of attending. Since she had enrolled at Albemarle, she had seldom attended services. She liked to say she would rather read Shakespeare than listen to another dry sermon.

The revival began with an early morning prayer meeting. With Lottie typically not in attendance, more than one young woman suggested that they pray for the conversion of Lottie Moon. When Lottie caught wind of this, she decided to play their game.

"I'll come to the meeting tonight and show you it won't make any difference," she boasted. "Furthermore, I'll show you all the flaws in the preacher's arguments and why no intelligent woman should spend another minute of her time in church!"

That evening Dr. Broadus, who had heard all about Albemarle's brilliant but obstinate scholar, happily spied Lottie sitting in the first pew. He had been praying more than usual about his sermon and about the enigma whose piercing blue eyes were riveted on him.

That evening, Lottie returned to her room in a troubled state. As she wrote later to a cousin, "I went to the service to scoff and returned to my room to pray all night."[1] The next morning she was sitting in the front pew again. She had not come to gloat or argue or embarrass the other young women. Rather, she came to praise her Lord and Savior, Jesus Christ. And she wouldn't be quiet about it, either. Jesus had won a powerful witness who was determined to devote her entire life to Him. How and where she would begin her Christian work were questions that would have to wait to be answered.

In 1861, Lottie Moon graduated from Albemarle. She was one of five women awarded the master of arts degree, equivalent to the degree awarded to Virginia's graduating men. No woman in the state of Virginia, or the entire South, had ever before soared to these heights of scholarship. As her cousin James liked to tease her, she was now one of the five most educated women in the world—or the world as he knew it.

Even though she was leaning toward entering the mission field, having been influenced by Dr. Broadus among others, the war prevented her from pursuing her dreams. On everyone's mind at the graduation ceremony was the cause of the Confederacy and the plight of Virginia's brave fighting men. Without hope of finding employment, Lottie returned home to Viewmont to tutor young Edmonia. Her only occasions to leave the estate were when Orianna, then a certified physician, asked for her help at a Charlottesville hospital. Wanting to aid the cause, Lottie accepted, bringing linen from Viewmont to cut up into bandages.

A gentle evening breeze caressed her cheek, waking Lottie from her foray into the past. She watched the lace curtains move in a slow rhythm, giving what she knew was a false sense of peace.

The war was over, but her family's trials were just beginning. *Or rather, trial,* she thought to herself, for everything that was about to happen to the Moons could be traced back to money. To accommodate the war effort, all their money had been converted into Confederate currency, which was now worthless. Without money, there was no way her mother could continue to manage Viewmont in its present state, even with her brother Isaac's help. (Her oldest brother, Thomas, who had become a physician, had died years earlier during a cholera epidemic.) It was only a matter of time before the slaves would acknowledge their freedom and go elsewhere.

Orianna would leave soon, too, and her sisters Colie, Mollie, and Edmonia had made plans to continue their education away from home. To finance their education and keep her mother afloat, land would have to be parceled off and sold. That would be the only solution.

And what would she do? Lately, given her success tutoring her sister, Lottie had decided she might be most valuable to the South as a teacher. Was that where God was leading her? He had certainly laid the way for her to obtain an excellent education. Only four other women in the entire South were as qualified as she to stand in front of a classroom. But what about her desire to serve God with her entire life?

Closing her eyes again, she began to pray before drifting back to sleep. This time her dreams were scenes from an old storybook—and she was Ann Judson.

THREE

There it was, more brilliant than she had imagined—the red Georgia clay. The train ride had been rather monotonous until now, but the sight of the rich farmland made Lottie sit up and take notice. She and Anna were almost there.

When the conductor bellowed, "Cartersville!" the two primly dressed young women instinctively reached for each other's hands.

"Do you see your cousin yet?" asked Anna.

As the train slowed to a stop at the depot, Lottie searched the waiting faces. "I'm sure I'll know him when I see him," she answered. "Anyway, I'm dying to get off this train and stretch my legs."

No sooner had the two women alighted than a red-faced, overweight man came bustling toward them. "Miss Lottie, let me help you with those bags," he said, wiping his brow with a handkerchief.

"Pleasant Moon! Your voice is the same, but I'd be hard pressed to pick you out of a crowd," Lottie said, laughing.

"And you must be Anna Safford," Pleasant said quickly, not forgetting his manners. "Lottie, I can't tell you what this means to have you here, teaching at the first Cartersville School for Girls!"

Lottie nodded, but something in her cousin's voice was setting off bells in her brain. "Why don't we drive by the school on our way to your house?" she suggested hopefully.

Pleasant looked everywhere but into her eyes. "Miss Lottie, well. . .oh well, I might as well just spit it out. The best we could do was an old cannery for the school building. Those Yankees went and burned everything else, and there just wasn't time or money to build."

Lottie put her hand on his arm. It was common knowledge that most Southern states had lost more than half their wealth during the war. "We've all been through the war, Pleasant. Viewmont is still standing, but it isn't an estate anymore."

"What about the students, Mr. Moon?" Anna asked. "How many girls are enrolled for the fall?"

Pleasant went on to tell the sad tale that only seven girls had enrolled. But it was June, and there were months before classes would start. There was plenty of time to recruit girls and fix up the building.

"That's what we're here for, Cousin," Lottie said, her voice conveying her strong spirit. "We didn't want to be anywhere else."

Since they had met each other four years earlier as fellow teachers at Kentucky's Danville Female Academy, Lottie and Anna had talked of running their own school someday. Moreover, even though Anna was a Presbyterian, the two women found they shared a strong desire to go into missions, too. But, first things first, Lottie decided. When Pleasant, a prominent businessman in Cartersville, wrote her about the proposed school, she and Anna agreed to come as soon as the current school year ended.

Using their own money and elbow grease, the two women had the cannery ready for the first day of class. Even though enrollment hadn't increased over the summer, by the second week, thirty girls were coming. After a few months, more than one hundred girls were enrolled. Anna and Lottie felt certain they were where God wanted them—for now.

As Lottie was ringing the last school bell of the year in June 1872, Edmonia Moon was sailing for China. Eddie was only twenty-one years old, but she had known for some time that she wanted to be a missionary. The biggest surprise for her older sister was how Eddie had convinced the Southern Baptist Missions Board to send an unmarried woman alone to China.

Since their mother's death in June 1870, Lottie and Eddie had spent many hours talking about missions. At the Richmond Female Institute, where she was a student and the secretary of missions, Eddie found herself in the unique position of corresponding with Southern Baptist missionaries, among them Tarleton and Martha Crawford in Tengchow, China. When Martha Crawford wrote of the need for single women to come to China, Eddie fired back a response. Would Martha write her a personal letter that she could present to the missions board, asking one Edmonia Moon to come to Tengchow?

Now Eddie's letters beckoned Lottie. After giving the matter some thought, Lottie wrote, "Our Lord does not call on women to preach, or to pray in public, but no less does He say to them than to men, 'Go, work in My fields.'"

In February 1873, Reverend R. B. Headden, pastor of the Cartersville Baptist Church, returned from a missions conference in rural Georgia. He was among a group of ministers who had pledged to return to their home churches to preach a single message: that the congregation pray to the Lord of the harvest to send more laborers to the mission field. When he stood before his congregation that first Sunday back in the pulpit, Reverend Headden looked as usual into the eyes of Lottie Moon, who was seated in the front pew next to her friend, Anna Safford.

Before giving the sermon, he had prayed privately that the Lord would send one person from his congregation to answer the call. When he finished the service, two women stood before him. "Lottie, Anna—" The pastor spread his hands wide, not knowing what to say to the single women he had come to treasure as invaluable members of his congregation.

"The call was as clear as a bell," Lottie piped up. "For some time, Reverend Headden, I've known I wanted to serve as a missionary in China. I am now ready to go—and so is Miss Safford."

Almost immediately Anna contacted the missions board of the Presbyterian church, while Lottie likewise wrote the Southern Baptists. She made it clear she wanted to serve with her sister Edmonia, who had written desperately of the need for more workers in Tengchow. When all the arrangements were made, in June 1873, Lottie and Anna informed Pleasant Moon and the girls and their parents at the Cartersville school of their decision to go. The reaction to their news was one of confusion and sadness. Why did they have to go all the way to China when they were needed in Georgia? Lottie could only tell them what she had poured out in all her missives to Edmonia: She was called to go.

Edmonia responded immediately to her sister's heart cry: "I know of no one who could fill your place here

[China]. In the first place not every one is willing to come to China. In the next place their having the proper qualifications is doubtful. . . . But after all, it is not for my sake I want you to come, but for the sake of the Chinese. I would not persuade you against what you think right."[1]

On July 7, 1873, Lottie received official notification that her application for appointment to North China had been approved by the Southern Baptist Missions Board. Support for her trip and tenure in Tengchow came not only from her church in Cartersville but also the Richmond Female Institute, as well as funds from her mother's will. After brief visits with family members, Lottie and Anna left Baltimore by train on August 18, arriving at the San Francisco station on August 30. The two would-be missionaries boarded the steamship *Costa Rica* on September 1, bound for Japan.

After twenty-five days at sea and almost as many spent suffering from seasickness, Lottie welcomed the sight of Yokohama's harbor. After docking in two more Japanese ports and two attempts to leave the port of Nagasaki, thanks to a hurricane, the battered ship finally arrived in Shanghai on October 7, 1873. Lottie was greeted warmly by the Crawfords and by Dr. and Mrs. Matthew Yates, who were long-time Southern Baptist missionaries in Shanghai. But it was also a time for more good-byes. Anna Safford would go from Shanghai to the Presbyterian mission in Suchow, just northwest of the bustling port of entry.

"Dr. Yates said you can send all letters to him and he'll forward them to me," Lottie told her, trying not to cry. "But don't say anything so important that it can't wait six months!"

"And we can always try to visit each other," Anna said, her own eyes filled with tears. "It seems like we've always been together, doesn't it?"

Lottie nodded, willing herself to remember their mission first, rather than their friendship. "Remember how the girls came to school, Anna. First there were seven, then there were thirty. We just have to trust God that He's leading us and we'll be all right."

The two friends hugged each other tightly and then walked away in different directions, sneaking occasional glances until both were swallowed up among the milling masses in a foreign land.

FOUR

To enter the ancient walled city of Tengchow, Lottie had to pass through one of four gates, each with a different meaning. The East Gate was known as "Birth of Spring," the South was called "Looking toward Heaven," the North Gate bore the title "To Go to the Sea," and the West was simply referred to as "Welcome Mercy." Perched overlooking the two-thousand-year-old fortress, the driver of the *shentze* wanted to make sure his new American passenger realized the importance of this moment. But all Lottie could think about was that her grueling two-day journey in this barrel-like contraption that was pulled by two donkeys was almost over.

After leaving Shanghai, Lottie and the Crawfords had sailed north to Chefoo in the province of Shantung, considered the most populated province in all of China. From there, the missionaries employed shentzes to take them the remaining fifty miles to Tengchow. After the jarring trip, Lottie thought every bone in her body must be fractured. What difference did it make what gate she went through as long as she was finally here?

Lottie eventually entered through the East Gate, but she wasn't at all sure her presence would bring a rebirth of any kind. In a city that numbered over eighty thousand residents, she was one of few "white-faced" people, and judging from the hostile looks she received, she was hardly welcome. For the last thirteen years, missionaries had been allowed in Tengchow by order of a foreign treaty. But as every missionary knew, being allowed and being welcomed were vastly different reactions.

Although there was only a handful of Southern Baptist missionaries in Tengchow, those workers in the harvest field had managed to establish two churches in the last decade. Dr. J. B. Hartwell, who had been among the first to arrive in 1860, was in charge of the North Street Church, while the Crawfords had organized what had come to be called the Monument Street Church in the southwest part of the city. Besides the two couples, Lottie was soon introduced to Sallie Holmes, who ran the school for girls near the Crawfords' home. Sallie had lost her husband and daughter in her early years in China but had stayed on with her young son, determined not to leave the field.

Lottie and Edmonia completed the Southern Baptist contingent. *We are two couples and three single women*, Lottie thought as she began to grasp the situation. *We are but tiny, flickering candles in a never-ending night, in a city where even a mountain—Temple Mountain—is thought to contain the good and evil spirits that control the peoples' destiny.*

Despite the bleak outlook in Tengchow, Lottie was thrilled to be with her sister again. "I just can't believe how well you speak the native dialects," Lottie said with pride over breakfast one morning. "You seem to have accomplished so much in such a short time."

Edmonia looked down at her plate, barely acknowledging her sister's words. "You must start with a language teacher right away, Lottie," she said quietly. "But knowing how you love languages, Mandarin shouldn't be a problem."

"And the boys' school that you're running? Martha and Sallie said how well you have done for such a young woman. Oh, how I wish Mama could see you here!" Lottie clapped her hands and then stopped at the sight of Eddie's down-turned face.

"Lottie, life is hard here, very hard. And I haven't been feeling well. I didn't want to scare you off since we need every bit of help we can get. But you can only go so far in one day, you can only teach so many lessons, and then there is much to do just to stay alive!" Eddie's face crinkled up as tears began flowing down her cheeks. Lottie quickly enveloped her sister in a hug, her heart breaking that Eddie had been bottling up these emotions for so long. Had there been no one for her sister to confide in?

Determined to make a difference not only for her sister and the other missionaries but for the Chinese people, Lottie threw herself into study and work. A language tutor, a man, was hired to help her learn Mandarin. Once a day he visited her at the Crawfords' home, pointing over and over again to Chinese characters with his long fingernails. At the same time, Lottie assisted Eddie at the school and Martha Crawford at her medical clinic. Sallie Holmes told her that as soon as she had mastered basic sentences, she could accompany her outside the walls of Tengchow. There were many villages where the gospel had never been preached and where no one had ever heard the name Jesus Christ.

Lottie watched as Martha and Eddie mounted their own individual sedan chairs hired for a ride into the country.

Grasping the bamboo poles, she then followed suit. She couldn't imagine riding for miles in a chair carried by four Chinese coolies. Sallie, riding on a mule, quickly came up alongside them.

"Once we've stopped at the market for our picnic supplies, we'll be on our way," Sallie said to Lottie. Lottie made a mental note to learn to ride a donkey in the near future. Sedan chair or shentze, neither one was her kind of transportation!

Leaving by the West Gate, the party of women made their way slowly to the first village, several miles away. Lottie felt relieved to leave the jumble of streets and formal ways of city life for a taste of the country. Riding out here with the green undulating hills and the mountains in the distance reminded her of her home in Virginia. Or, what once was her home.

As they passed through the village gates, the women were quickly swarmed by men who gave them hateful looks and muttered things under their breath. "What are they saying?" Lottie asked Martha, who rode in the chair beside her.

"They're calling us foreign devils," Martha said. "Don't worry—they're just repeating what they've been told. The women will give us a much warmer reception."

Sure enough, once Sallie and Martha had found a place to stop and began producing plates of food, the women of the village scurried over, their children right behind them. The villagers wanted to touch Lottie's curls and her silk dress, to examine her food, and just to stare at her for long periods of time. "What should I do?" Lottie cried to Edmonia. "Do I just sit here?"

Edmonia nodded. "Yes, Lottie. And smile. We're going to start our lesson now. Try to follow along in Mandarin if you can."

After passing out hymn sheets written in Mandarin, the missionary women began leading the songs, and soon most of the village women were joining in singing. Lottie could only stare in amazement. In the villages, the women seemed so open to hearing the gospel message. They weren't relegated to their own private courtyards, as they were in Tengchow, kept out of view of society.

Not wanting to wear out their welcome, Martha, Eddie, and Sallie soon gathered up their belongings and left the village. "Let's keep going," Sallie encouraged. But after visiting a second village, the sun was getting low in the sky and they decided to return home. Though exhausted, Lottie felt exhilarated at the same time. In a country village was where she could make a difference, she thought to herself. *Someday, I pray, God will lead me to such a place.*

Although Edmonia had informed Lottie that her health was poor, Lottie wasn't too worried about her younger sister. She had noticed Eddie's persistent cough, but she thought it would go away soon. After all, Eddie was in her early twenties, more than ten years younger than Lottie. Lottie thought she was probably trying to make a good impression on the Crawfords by doing more than any first-time missionary.

When Eddie suggested that they go to another village in the early winter of 1875 to hold church services, Lottie eagerly agreed. Obviously, her sister was feeling strong enough to make such a journey, and the idea of winning Chinese converts had added color to her cheeks. "This is the village of a woman who used to live in Tengchow," Eddie said. "She has tried to explain her new faith to her family and friends, but she needs our help."

When the Moon sisters entered the village, accompanied by Sallie Holmes and Martha Crawford, they received no hostile looks or verbal threats. Instead, they were bombarded with questions that their family member was unable to answer. Separating the curious villagers into groups, the missionary women passed out new pages of hymns written in Mandarin, as well as testimonials about Jesus. Lottie was able to open her Bible and read Jesus' words in their native dialect. After one year in China, her command of the language was impressive, winning even the praise of Martha Crawford.

Lottie and Edmonia stayed several days in the village, not wanting to leave until they had established a place of worship and put the few new Chinese Christians in charge of holding simple services. They promised to return soon or to send another missionary in the next few months. But after returning to Tengchow, Lottie knew they wouldn't be making any trips in the near future. Pale and feverish, Eddie had gone straight to bed.

The diagnosis was typhoid fever, but she soon developed symptoms of pneumonia, as well. Mentally, Eddie was changing, too. The harsh climate of northern China, the unending workload, and her own impossibly high expectations were given as reasons by Tengchow doctors for her nervous breakdown. Lottie suspected another reason, too. The Southern Baptist missionaries were not getting along with each other, and often Eddie and Lottie found themselves caught in the middle of arguments. Moreover, living in Tarleton Crawford's house—an odd structure with an imperious tower that offended the Chinese—had spawned rumors that Eddie and Lottie were his second and third wives.

As Eddie's physical symptoms abated, Lottie was able to find new lodging for them at the residence of Dr. Hartwell, who had left China to seek medical help for his wife. The change proved to be good medicine, for a while.

Even so, when the Crawfords returned from a brief furlough in Japan, Lottie insisted that Edmonia go to Shanghai to stay with Dr. and Mrs. Yates. Lottie tried to reassure herself that in a larger city with a more temperate climate and the care of a physician, Edmonia was sure to return to her old self. In the fall of 1876, however, Lottie received a telegram to come immediately to Shanghai. Edmonia's devastating symptoms, both physical and mental, had returned. Dr. Yates and the other missionaries had decided the best course was to send her home.

Three days before Christmas Eve 1876, the sisters arrived at Viewmont and Edmonia was quickly put to bed. Upon Lottie's request, Orie was there, as were other local doctors. There was little they could do for her but to prescribe cod liver oil and bed rest. Lottie was pleased to see her sister improving as the months went by.

With Edmonia on the mend, Lottie started making inquiries about when she could return to Tengchow alone. Rumors were adrift that perhaps she should never have been sponsored if she were likely to return home so quickly. Although the Crawfords had taken a brief furlough, missionaries were expected to remain in the field indefinitely. When Lottie informed the Southern Baptist Missions Board that they could book her immediate passage back to China, she was given an answer she didn't expect. The board was in debt; there was no money to pay for her transportation.

The situation was resolved when the Women's Missionary Society of the First Baptist Church of Richmond came to Lottie's rescue. They had been contributing to a fund to provide housing for Lottie and Edmonia, having heard of the sisters' less-than-ideal living situation. Now they asked if they could use the money to pay for Lottie's passage back to China.

Almost a year to the day she left Shanghai, Lottie arrived back in China. She wrote exultantly to the missions board, as if assuring them of her dedication: "It is almost worthwhile to go away from China for awhile to get the hearty welcome one receives on returning. I sometimes think that missionaries are the warmest hearted people in the world!"[1] Before returning to Tengchow, she managed to spend a few days with Anna Safford in nearby Suchow. Then, sailing to Chefoo, she was warmly greeted by Presbyterian missionaries who secured her transportation back home. This time of year, the safest way to reach Tengchow was by mule train.

Lottie Moon arrived at the Crawfords' home on Christmas Eve 1877. On her two trips to Tengchow, she had survived first a hurricane and now a snowstorm. Once she had shed her numerous layers of clothing and held a mug of tea in her hands, she felt her old self again. Truly, she thought, she belonged here with the Chinese people, and so did her fellow workers. The missionaries' numbers were few, but their determination could not be measured.

FIVE

"Miss Moon expects to open a boarding school for girls of the higher class," reported the *Foreign Mission Journal* in 1877, much to the delight of women in Richmond and Cartersville who knew of Lottie's gift of teaching. But as she had experienced at the fledgling school in Georgia, Lottie was finding it difficult to entice girls to come.

Girls of higher classes were trained at home and then given away in marriage at an early age to a prearranged husband. Those girls of the lower classes were required to work to support their families or, much worse, forced into a life of prostitution. It was from the lower classes that Lottie secured her first class of boarding students, all five of them.

Even though North China was suffering from a devastating famine, Lottie opened her school in early 1878 at Dr. Hartwell's former residence. As the school's only teacher and supervisor, she would teach, clothe, cook for, and nurse these girls all by herself. Sallie, who had taught school for many years, was happy to lend her teaching materials, as was Martha Crawford.

With finances tighter than usual due to the famine and the perpetual deficit of the missions budget, Lottie launched into her first letter-writing campaign to her faithful supporters in the United States. "For fifteen dollars a year you can support one of my girls," she wrote. "Rest assured, I will be reporting to you on your girl's progress, academically and spiritually." The need became greater when, at the end of the first year, thirteen girls were enrolled.

When the girls were not at the school, Lottie was free to pursue what she had come to realize was her deepest desire. She could travel to the villages again. Sallie Holmes, who had sent her only son back to the United States to attend school, was always a willing partner.

After a full day at a village they had visited earlier, Sallie whispered to Lottie a change of plans. "One of the coolies has a relative in the village. He says we can spend the night there."

Lottie's eyes opened wide. To have a "foreign devil" stay overnight in a villager's house was sure to bring the wrath of the evil spirits. But maybe this was the opening they were praying for, the opportunity to keep sharing their message.

Mats were rolled out on top of the *kangs,* four-foot-high mud-brick rectangles that were the only sources of heat in a village home. Reluctantly, Lottie lay down on the kang, aware that many pairs of eyes were on her. Sallie lay next to her, her eyes already closed. When they awoke the next morning, they noticed holes had been cut through the soot-stained paper windows so that villagers could more closely observe them. At breakfast in the room that adjoined the one where they slept, thirty villagers were gathered, eager for Lottie and Sallie to open their "heavenly book."

Until Sallie returned to the United States in 1881, she

and Lottie traveled hundreds of miles together, visiting almost as many villages. Lottie wrote often of her experiences, saying, "As I wander from village to village, I feel it is no idle fancy that the Master walks beside me, and I hear His voice saying gently, 'I am with you always, even unto the end.'"

But once again there were those voices, echoing from American church newspapers, that wished to minimize the efforts expended by Lottie Moon and others in the field. As she had put pen to paper to rally support for her school, Lottie wrote furiously in response to an article that declared there was no such thing as "missionary hardship." She had lost her sister to the rigors of the mission field, and she could point to many others with similar stories. Dr. Hartwell had lost two wives, and now Tarleton Crawford was recuperating in the United States after suffering a nervous breakdown.

"I am always ashamed to dwell on physical hardships. To speak in the open air in a foreign tongue from six to eleven times a day is no trifle. If anyone fancies sleeping on brick beds in a room with dirt floors and walls blackened by the smoke of many generations, the yard also being the stable yard and the stable itself being within three feet of your door, I wish to declare most emphatically. . .I find it most unpleasant."[1]

In 1882 Lottie decided, with the approval of the missions board, to close the boarding school. An outbreak of a highly contagious disease had made her fearful for the safety of the girls, and she sent them home. The school had been a success, with almost forty enrolled at the time of its closing, but Lottie was near the end of her rope. She could not do everything for every girl by herself and minister to others as well. With Tarleton Crawford gone, she and Martha were the only Southern Baptist missionaries supposedly serving all of North China!

Lying on her kang at night, she couldn't stop thinking of the poor, illiterate women in the villages she loved to visit. If only the missions board could persuade more men and women to come as missionaries, she could feel free to travel again. Was that unreasonable to wish for? She surely wasn't trading one set of dire circumstances for the ease of another. No, God had planted this seed in her heart for a reason.

Besides, Lottie Moon had a dream she hadn't shared with anyone—except God.

By December 1885, Lottie's dream was on the minds of many.

Lottie herself had just arrived in Pingtu, 120 miles inland from Tengchow. And two new Southern Baptist missionary couples were in Hwanghsien, just twenty miles from their home base. Lottie's dream to establish a chain of mission stations from Tengchow all the way to the interior of China was being realized.

What had happened, Lottie knew, was an answer to prayer. Here she was, after all, in this remote but populated outpost, the only white woman the people of Pingtu had ever seen. She was also the first Southern Baptist woman to open a new mission.

One month ago she had made the trip to Pingtu for the first time, a trip that took four days and three nights—nights spent in the filthiest and most miserable inns she had ever experienced. She could still feel the rats crawling on her feet, the lice running wild across the rest of her body. But when she reached Pingtu, the people seemed friendly and open to learn about God. What they needed were supplies, food, and medicine, and enough material written in Mandarin so she could reach them. Thus, she had returned to Tengchow briefly and then made the harrowing trip again—without the blessing of the U.S. North China consul. He had given Lottie a stern warning that she would not be protected so far inland since no foreigners resided there.

She had not, however, come alone. A Christian Chinese couple from Tengchow, the Chaos, accompanied her. One of Mr. Chao's relatives was willing to rent a house to him, acting for Lottie, for twenty-four dollars for the year, even though she was only planning to stay until summer. No Chinese man would dare rent his house directly to a foreigner.

As she was emptying her belongings from one of her trunks, she turned to Mrs. Chao, who was busy putting fresh paper on the windows of the rented house. "Since I'm going to be living here for a while, I don't want to act like I do when I enter villages just for a day," Lottie said. "I want to seem as if I am a native to the village."

"First, you must begin to dress as a woman of Pingtu," Mrs. Chao suggested slyly. "Then you wait inside your house for the village to come to you."

Impatient and impetuous as always, Lottie didn't like waiting long. But she didn't want to leave the house, either. Digging inside another trunk, she found a leather-bound journal and held it high as if in triumph. She then went to the room of the house where she did her cooking and went to work. A few hours later, distinctly foreign odors began emanating outside, causing the villagers to take notice. While the adults of the village were able to restrain themselves, the children were not. They came running inside Lottie's house, and she was there to meet them with a freshly baked batch of Anna Maria's tea cakes.

Women and men started coming, too. First they ate

tea cakes and chatted with Lottie in their native dialect. Then, weeks later, she turned the conversation into a discussion about the One who had changed her life. She also began distributing the song sheets and tracts she had brought with her from Tengchow. Tears came to Lottie's eyes when the children were finally able to sing "Jesus Loves Me," one of her favorite songs. When Lottie wanted to go visiting, Mrs. Chao was an invaluable asset, since she was able to introduce Lottie to her neighbors and help her organize Christian classes for the women.

As spring approached, comfortable in her new status as Pingtu resident, Lottie was able to leave the city gates and visit other villages. She looked and talked like a native, but what she said was strange but appealing. One of her first stops was ten miles away at the village of Sha-ling. A Chinese Christian named Dan Ho Bang, who had been converted months earlier by the missionaries at Hwanghsien, eagerly awaited her arrival at his home village.

June 1886 found Lottie back in Tengchow, furiously writing letters once again. Her first concern was that the missions board send more missionaries to Pingtu, as well as Hwanghsien. Illness had claimed the lives of two of the new missionaries, leaving only one man remaining at the latter station. But her heart was with and for the people of Pingtu: "We must go out and live among them, manifesting the spirit of our Lord. We need to make friends before we can hope to make converts."

To provide for new missionaries, Lottie had come up with a plan. She had read how Methodist churchwomen annually collected an offering for missions. Why couldn't Southern Baptist women do likewise? Before she returned to Pingtu in April 1887, she penned the following plea, asking that an offering be taken during the week before Christmas.

"Need it be said why the week before Christmas is chosen? Is not the festive season, when families and friends exchange gifts in memory of The Gift laid on the altar of the world for the redemption of the human race, the most appropriate time to consecrate a portion from abounding riches and scant poverty to send forth the good tidings of great joy into all the earth?"

So that the funds would not be raised by gimmickry, she offered these stern and solemn words:

> *I wonder how many of us really believe that it is more blessed to give than to receive. A woman who accepts that statement of our Lord Jesus Christ as a fact. . .will make giving a principle of her life. She will lay aside sacredly not less than one-tenth of her income or her earnings as the Lord's money, which she would no more dare touch for personal use than she would steal. How many there are among our women, alas, who imagine that because "Jesus paid it all," they need pay nothing, forgetting that the prime object of their salvation was that they should follow in the footsteps of Jesus Christ!*[2]

Lottie wouldn't know the results of her letter until she returned again to Tengchow—if only she could hang on until then. She was in her late forties, but she could feel her robust health deteriorating. North China had a way of doing that to missionaries.

Sallie Holmes's departing had created a void, but it had also filled a need. Eager for a place that she could call her own, and one that could also serve as a meeting place for missionaries, Lottie was thrilled when she was allowed to move into her dear friend's home, which actually consisted of three three-hundred-year-old houses enclosed inside a mud wall. While she had spent most of her time since 1885 in Pingtu, Lottie looked forward to her few months in Tengchow when she could relax at the compound that had been christened "Little Crossroads."

In July 1889, when temperatures soared to well over one hundred degrees in Pingtu, Lottie once again sought refuge at Little Crossroads. Her mail was overflowing with good news. Because of the success of the first women's offering before Christmas 1887, there was now enough money to support missionaries to North China, and even one to serve in Pingtu! Then came the letter from the missions board for which she had prayed. Once Lottie had sufficiently indoctrinated this new helper into the life of the village, she was finally free to leave on her first furlough since she had taken her sister home.

Or so she thought.

But when Lottie and Fannie Knight, the new missionary from North Carolina, arrived in Pingtu in early 1890, they were greeted with dubious news.

"Two women from Sha-ling are here to see you, Moo La Dee," a villager greeted Lottie as she passed through the village gates.

As she entered her house, the two women were sitting there, tears running down their faces. "We have come to be baptized, Moo La Dee. We believe in the heavenly book and all that Dan Ho-bang has taught us."

Lottie smiled at them. "But why are you crying?" she asked.

The women at first were hesitant to answer. Finally, one spoke softly. "Because we are about to be married and our husbands are not Christians. They will want us to worship their Buddhist ancestors, and we only worship the one true God."

Lottie quickly sent for a minister from Hwanghsien to come perform the baptisms. At the same time, she made plans to go to Sha-ling herself. The Chinese New Year was fast approaching, and she sensed trouble for the small but strong group of believers there. Among them, she knew, were an uncle and his nephew, Li-Qin and Li Show-ting, who had already endured great persecution for their faith. By reading a copy of the New Testament that Lottie had given his uncle, Li Show-ting had come to believe in Jesus himself. Along with Dan Ho-bang, the Lis had been the mainstays of the tiny Sha-ling church.

Before she could leave Pingtu, though, a loud cry went up at the village gate. Men, women, and children hurried to the edge of the village where a man lay, almost unconscious. When Lottie finally was able to see the man for herself, she knew him right away. It was Li Show-ting, barely alive from a savage beating, his scalp hanging from his head. Soon another messenger arrived from Sha-ling. Could Lottie come right away? Dan Ho-bang was also being tortured for his faith.

Lottie knew she couldn't wait for help to come. Leaving Fannie at Pingtu, she ordered a shentze to take her to Sha-ling. Being a Christian meant enduring persecution, or so she had once told Dan. She couldn't run away from her faith now, even if she was a single woman.

The scene at Sha-ling was worse than she could have imagined. There was Dan Ho-bang, strung onto bamboo poles, streams of blood coursing down his body. She ran immediately to his side, relieved to see that he was still, somehow, alive. "Don't be afraid, Dan," she whispered in Chinese. "You have believed and you will be saved. Remember Jesus' words—'Blessed are you who are persecuted in My name!'"

"Get away from him, foreign devil!" one young man shouted at Lottie, lifting his sword in the air.

Calmly and with an assurance that was not her own, Lottie turned to face him. *Soon the sword will pierce my body*, she thought as a strange smile crossed her face. *But then I will see Jesus*. Her gaze never left his as he began to lower his weapon with both hands as if to slice her in two. Suddenly, to the amazement of the watching crowd, the sword clattered to the ground and the man's arms hung limply by his side. He looked at the diminutive white woman, his eyes pools of disbelief.

She would take Dan Ho-bang back to Pingtu with her until he had fully recovered. When he returned months later to Sha-ling, he was amazed to find the tiny church bursting with new converts. Those he spoke with were impressed that a white woman would give her life for a Chinese man. And then they had heard about the sacrifice of Jesus.

In the summer of 1891, Lottie finally sailed back to the United States. Although Viewmont had been sold, Eddie was still living in Virginia, in the town of Scottsville. After resting six months at Eddie's home, Lottie acceded to the numerous requests by church groups and missions organizations for her time and presence. By October 1893, she was ready to return, having received encouraging letters from Fannie Knight in Pingtu and others in the field.

In few words she summarized her desire to go back. Whenever asked, she said, "China is my home." She did not say Tengchow or Little Crossroads or Pingtu or Sha-ling. That was because Lottie Moon had a new goal. She wanted to be the first missionary to visit two hundred villages in a church quarter—eight hundred villages in a year.

SIX

The cannonball had traveled through the mud wall around Little Crossroads, through the wall of the house where Lottie lived, and out of the back wall of her bedroom. Lottie was on her way back from Pingtu when the war came to her doorstep, but even holes in her bedroom wouldn't make her leave Tengchow.

While many missionaries fled China during the Sino-Japanese War of 1894, Lottie used the opportunity to spread the gospel. She received more Chinese visitors at Little Crossroads than ever before, troubled citizens of Tengchow and outside villages who needed to hear some good news. The result of the war, though, boded ill for foreign missionaries and for Chinese Christians who, according to popular belief, had accepted whatever "foreign devils" taught them.

The treaty that ended the war stipulated that China open up several ports to foreign trade, as well as allow Japan to build factories in China. Much to the Chinese government's displeasure, Western countries soon agreed to an "open door policy" that gave them equal rights to encroach upon China as well. In a few years an antiforeign feeling had spread through the Chinese population, a sense of outrage that was to be embodied in the Boxer Uprising.

Lottie had already written to the United States consul in North China about her premonition that something terrible was about to happen. While awaiting a response, she continued supervising various schools in Tengchow, teaching Sunday school, and trying to visit two villages every day, ever aware that hostilities were increasing. One winter morning in early 1900, the war again came to her doorstep.

She almost jumped out of her chair in the kitchen as a young Chinese man, out of breath and worn from a long journey, collapsed on her floor. "You are Moo La Dee, yes?" he said after a minute or so, when he regained his composure.

Lottie nodded, then went to fix her guest a cup of tea to speed his story along.

"You must come with me to Pingtu right away. I am sent by Pastor Li Show-ting."

At the mention of Li's name Lottie smiled. Under his supervision there were now thriving churches in both Sha-ling and Pingtu. But that was before the Boxers, or the "Righteous and Harmonious Fists," began terrorizing North China. They had been given free rein by the Chinese government to kill foreign missionaries and Chinese Christians, as well as destroy all signs of foreign influence.

"What has happened in Pingtu?" Lottie asked, almost not wanting to know the answer.

The young man proceeded to tell an almost familiar story. Thirteen Chinese Christians were being tortured by Boxer supporters when Pastor Li intervened on their behalf, and now they were lying in a prison in Pingtu. Many were asking for her to come.

The unspoken question was how she could make such

a journey at a time like this. Lottie thought for a moment. "Can you get me a shentze like the ones Chinese magistrates use?"

A few hours later, Lottie called out to her waiting guide that she was ready to leave. "Boxers are standing in groups at each of the gates of Tengchow," he announced, and then his mouth dropped open at the sight of the missionary.

Not only would she be traveling in a dignitary's transport, but Lottie would also be dressed the part. Her long, dark hair had been slicked back from her forehead and braided in a queue. Heavily embroidered robes concealed her body. Squinting her blue eyes, she peered from side to side in the manner of the most imperious ruler.

"Well? Do you think I can pass?" she asked in perfect Mandarin. Her guide simply bowed and raced outside to wake up the waiting donkeys.

Along the way, the shentze with the heavy curtains was simply waved on by the Boxers they encountered. Not one Boxer dared to peer inside the esteemed traveling chamber, and there were many opportunities.

When she arrived in Pingtu, Lottie was greeted warmly by Pastor Li.

"The prisoners have all been released, Moo La Dee," he said. "But they still want to see you."

Lottie spent the next few days praying with and encouraging the persecuted Christians. But when the Boxers threatened Pingtu again, Lottie decided she must leave. To stay would put the villagers in even greater danger.

When Lottie arrived back in Tengchow, the situation was only slightly better. By July 1900, all missionaries were ordered to evacuate the city. Sailing on a gunboat from Tengchow harbor, Lottie and the other missionaries eventually reached Shanghai. From there, they were taken to Fukuoka, Japan, to wait out the conflict. Lottie, who was staying with Southern Baptist missionaries, was able to find a job teaching English during this unplanned furlough. Since she had no textbook, Lottie used the best book she could think of—the Bible.

In April 1901, Lottie and the others returned. Again, China had been defeated—this time by an international contingent—and the Boxers were no more. Lottie had anguished over the deaths of the many missionaries and now she could see the devastation firsthand. But even though Tengchow, Pingtu, and Sha-ling had been hit especially hard, Lottie could sense a new mood among the Chinese people. Because of the courageous stands of the foreign missionaries and Chinese Christians, there was a fervent desire to hear the gospel—and there were more missionaries coming to North China than ever before!

Over the years, Lottie had seen missionaries come and go, often not by choice. Even Fannie Knight, whom Lottie had come to treasure, had succumbed to illness and then death at a young age. But since the Boxer Uprising, Lottie felt hopeful. Dr. Thomas Ayers, a medical doctor and missionary, had arrived, as well as a registered nurse. Licking her lips, she knew what the subject of her next letter-writing campaign to the missions board would be: raising funds to build a hospital in Hwanghsien, where Dr. Ayers would be stationed.

Years earlier she had written begging for furloughs for missionaries, and her request had been honored. But when she, now the senior missionary in North China, received notice from the board that it was time to take another furlough, Lottie was caught by surprise. Ten years had passed since she had last seen Eddie. Although she had much to do in China, she felt a tug on her heart to go home. The year would pass quickly.

On February 27, 1904, as Lottie watched the San Francisco harbor slip away into a mist of nothingness, she felt, and looked, much older than her sixty-three years. Her furlough had been a decidedly bittersweet experience. While she had cared for her ailing brother, Isaac, in Virginia, she had also had the wonderful opportunity to see her late sister Orianna's grown sons. And while she had sat across the dinner table at Monticello from President Theodore Roosevelt—the two were among the honored guests at the University of Virginia's commencement exercises—she couldn't erase from her mind the picture of her decrepit sister. Eddie had sold her house and was now living in a boardinghouse, her grasp on reality tenuous.

Wasn't it time for her to retire? friends often asked her during the furlough. Shaking her head, Lottie always replied, "Oh, don't say that you don't want me to return. Nothing could make me stay. China is my joy and my delight. It is my home now."[1]

In early 1911 Lottie played host at Little Crossroads to women from three missionary societies. They were the first to organize the Women's Missionary Union of North China, and they had decided to elect Lottie as the first president.

Reporting on the efforts of the Southern Baptists, Lottie was aglow with the news. Where could she begin? They had sixteen churches in North China and fifty-six schools that had an enrollment of over a thousand students. Over two thousand Chinese Christians had been baptized. There was even a hospital and theological school in Hwanghsien and another hospital planned farther inland. When she spoke of the progress in the inland villages, Lottie's eyes shone with pride. In Sha-ling, Pastor Li had told her, what was once a Buddhist temple had been converted into a school.

Concerning the schools in Tengchow, Lottie spoke passionately of the progress missionaries had made toward eliminating the custom of binding girls' feet. Because of the great need for more schools, at her own expense she had recently opened another school at Little Crossroads. The only shadow Lottie could detect but didn't verbalize was the Southern Baptist missions budget. As always, she wished American churchgoers could spend a day with her just to see how valuable their contributions could be.

This new sense of optimism at the women's meeting could be sensed in China's political atmosphere, too. Lottie had followed keenly the career of Sun Yat-sen, a baptized Christian, who wanted to overthrow the stifling Manchu government of China and establish a republic. Since the Sino-Japanese War, he had been traveling widely in Western countries, trying to develop a government model for China. Now he was back in China, and many felt, correctly, that the revolution was at hand.

When the revolution started, the missionaries were again thrust into another life-or-death situation. Because Little Crossroads was a haven for all kinds of visitors, Lottie wasn't too surprised to see armed soldiers on her doorstep.

"There's been a great deal of vandalism in the neighborhood, Miss Lottie," one soldier said. "The fighting is going to start soon, too. Please take this gun for your own safety."

Lottie grimaced at the sight of the weapon. "No, thank you," she said. "I'll be all right." She didn't want to tell him that unless Little Crossroads were set ablaze, she had no plans to leave Tengchow.

Her stoicism would be put to the test. When the United States consul asked that all foreign missionaries vacate their stations for Chefoo, considered a safer port city, Lottie stayed put. Or at least that was what the other missionaries thought she was doing.

Meanwhile, in Hwanghsien, twenty miles away, the missionaries at the hospital had received similar instructions. Before leaving for Chefoo, Dr. Ayers, the head of the hospital, put Dr. Chu, his assistant, in charge. He left his office locked, even though he trusted that Dr. Chu would not enter the one room where he kept his personal files.

As Dr. Ayers and the others were waiting out the revolution in Chefoo, they couldn't help wondering what was happening at the hospital. In times of war, the hospital was an extremely busy place. After agonizing about Dr. Chu and the other Chinese hospital workers, Dr. Ayers decided to return to Hwanghsien. The roads were unsafe for anyone, but if an American were caught by a Manchu soldier, his life was in great peril.

When he finally arrived at Hwanghsien, after traveling mostly at night, Dr. Ayers found the hospital functioning perfectly and smoothly. There were wounded soldiers being treated in every available corner, but there was no lack of supplies or workers. Everyone was where he or she was supposed to be. And then Dr. Ayers saw something that he couldn't believe—the door was open to his office! *How could Dr. Chu have done this?* he thought, and then he saw the reason.

Sitting in his chair with a smile on her face was Lottie Moon. The doctor rubbed his eyes in disbelief. She and the other nurses were wrapping bandages in his office. As if it were obvious, Lottie said, "This was the only available room, Dr. Ayers. I hope you don't mind."

"But how did you get here? Why did you come?"

Lottie fastened her wizened gaze on the doctor. "When

I learned you had left, I had to come. There were Christians here who needed my help."

Now that the doctor had arrived, Lottie knew it was time to go home. The revolution was still going on, but Lottie wasn't worried about getting to Little Crossroads. An officer in Sun Yat-sen's army, the father of one of her students, had promised her safe passage. The message had been sent all the way to Tengchow. Lottie would sleep in her own bed that night.

SEVEN

I enclose to you the official statement about the famine in Central China. Will you not speak to the pastor of your church and ask him to obtain a contribution to help these poor sufferers?" Lottie wrote to her nephew in early 1912. "One cent, United States money, a day, up to the next harvest, will save a life! Unless help comes, and that speedily, from one to three million men, women, and children must perish from hunger."[1]

Although the revolution was over and Sun Yat-sen's army had claimed victory, the people of North China were hardly celebrating. A famine that had started four years earlier in the interior had spread slowly toward the north and was now enveloping the entire area from Pingtu to Tengchow. On the heels of the famine had come waves of smallpox and even bubonic plague. Little Crossroads, once a hostel for missionaries, had become a home for the ill and homeless.

This was the first year that no entry marked "Albemarle" would be made on the ledgers of the Southern Baptist Missions Board. Since the missions board could not send any money to help her, Lottie was withholding her contribution to help those around her. Mostly, she gave to the Christians in Pingtu. A report in November 1912 described how hundreds there were on the verge of starvation. *Thousands will die without a chance to know Jesus Christ,* Lottie thought to herself. She found herself succumbing to the dreaded enemy of missionaries—depression.

Writing in her dwindling bankbook, she scribbled, "I pray that no missionary will ever be as lonely as I have been."

By December, her fellow missionaries in Tengchow were seriously alarmed. Not only was she suffering from melancholy, but Lottie was much thinner than she had ever been. They quickly summoned a doctor from Hwanghsien. When he arrived, he had seen too many like her to fail to make an accurate diagnosis. Lottie Moon was, quite simply, starving herself to death. She had been giving away all her food and all her money to ease the crisis of the famine. It was reported that she weighed only fifty pounds.

Shortly before Christmas, Lottie was placed on a boat bound for Japan, under the care of a nurse. When the boat docked at Kobe on Christmas Eve, the nurse noticed that Lottie, who had been in a semiconscious state, began stirring. A day earlier, Lottie had surprised her by singing "Jesus Loves Me," her voice failing often. She had also asked the nurse to pray for her. Now Lottie began whispering, in Chinese, the names of those friends who had gone to heaven before her. With each name, her thin hands clasped together, then unclasped, in the Chinese form of greeting. After raising her hands a final time, Lottie Moon died. She had whispered no name at the end. The nurse, a Christian, assumed she was greeting her Lord at last.

Her ashes would be interred next to her brother's grave in

Crewe, Virginia. By her grave a spruce tree was planted by the Women's Missionary Union of Virginia and a headstone was placed. "Forty years a missionary of Southern Baptist Convention in China," the headstone reads, "Faithful Unto Death."

And on the street where Little Crossroads once stood, there is a marker in the shape of an obelisk. The monument, which is inscribed in Chinese characters, reads, "A monument to bequeath the love of Miss Lottie Moon, an American missionary." Below that line are the words "The Tengchow church remembers forever."

Although the gold and silver in the buried pillowcases was somehow never recovered, the treasure that was Lottie Moon is remembered yearly. Since 1918 when the Christmas Offering was named for her, more than two billion dollars has been collected to benefit overseas missions and support thousands of Lottie's fellow missionaries.

NOTES

Barbour Publishing, Inc., expresses its appreciation to all those who generously gave permission to reprint copyrighted material. Diligent effort has been made to identify, locate, contact, and secure permission to use copyrighted material. If any permissions or acknowledgments have been inadvertently omitted or if such permissions were not received by the time of publication, the publisher would sincerely appreciate receiving complete information so that correct credit can be given in future editions.

Chapter Two
1. Una Roberts Lawrence, *Lottie Moon* (Nashville, Tenn.: Sunday School Board of the Southern Baptist Convention, 1927), 45.

Chapter Three
1. Lawrence, 64.

Chapter Four
1. Lawrence, 84.

Chapter Five
1. Janet Benge and Geoff Benge, *Lottie Moon: Giving Her All for China* (Seattle, Wash.: YWAM Publishing, 2001), 116–17.
2. John Allen Moore, *The Life of Lottie Moon* (International Mission Board, 2001). Used by permission of the International Mission Board, SBC.

Chapter Six
1. Moore.

Chapter Seven
   1. Lawrence, 304.

SUGGESTED READING

Benge, Janet, and Geoff Benge, *Lottie Moon: Giving Her All for China*. Seattle, Wash.: YWAM Publishing, 2001.

Lawrence, Una Roberts, *Lottie Moon*. Nashville, Tenn.: Sunday School Board of the Southern Baptist Convention, 1927.

McPherson, James M., *Battle Cry of Freedom: The Civil War Era*. New York: Ballantine Books, 1989.

Tucker, Ruth A., *From Jerusalem to Irian Jaya: A Biographical History of Christian Missions*. Grand Rapids, Mich.: Zondervan, 1983.

NATE SAINT

ONE

Sioux City, Iowa—August 1943

Another hot and humid Iowa day, Nate thought, sitting on his army bunk, his thin T-shirt sticking to his skin. Even at this early hour, he could feel the temperature rising by the minute. Still, sultry or storming, there was no weather pattern conceived that could ruin his day. A smile lighting up his face, he said a quick prayer and finished dressing. This is the day that the Lord hath made! What a day to be alive!

Today, Friday, August 27, 1943, was the day Nate had waited for since he entered the Army Air Corps eight months earlier. Today was the final day of training before Saturday's announcement of the next class of those chosen to be in the Air Cadet Training Program. Those chosen few would be the army's newest fliers, receiving hundreds of hours of flying time, thanks to the good ol' United States government. So far his reviews had been good, and Nate thought he had a shot at making the program.

There was just one more hurdle—a rigorous hike to test the candidates' stamina. But with what he had been through, that should be a walk in the park. Since he had enlisted, he had endured a steady diet of lectures and drilling, not to mention moving. Being in the army was like being on a local bus that made too many stops. So far he had been stationed in camps on Long Island; Las Vegas, New Mexico; Santa Monica, California; the Mojave Desert; and St. Louis, Missouri. He knew this stint at Morningside College in Sioux City was just another temporary training exercise.

His boots laced up, Nate got into line with the others waiting outside. Already he could feel rivers of perspiration running down his face and chest, not to mention a familiar pain in his right leg. Slapping himself mentally, he focused his attention on the course ahead. He needed to be sharp and look sharp!

As the men hiked up and down hills, accelerating to meet the demands of the sergeant, Nate could see that he was lagging behind. Some of his friends gave him encouraging looks, and he forced his body to move faster. Hours later, he finished with the group, thinking only of his thin army bunk.

Entering the barracks, Nate said a quick prayer, thanking God that he was alone. There was something he had to do, and he didn't want company. Raising up his right pant leg, he looked at the familiar scar. The pain in his right leg had not been a fluke. The scar had reddened noticeably and was tender to the touch. He noticed that the glands in his groin were swollen, too. Nate didn't need a doctor to make a diagnosis. That had been done already, six years ago.

The next doctor he saw, courtesy of the army, would make sure—not out of spite but because of regulations—that he never flew a day as a cadet. Chronic osteomyelitis—an infection of the bone—required immediate medical care. The condition would prevent him from ever seeing combat action as a pilot. As more men entered the barracks, Nate decided he would see a doctor in the morning. Until then he would try to act as normal as possible. The hours passed slowly.

"G'night, Nate," one buddy called. Then—lights out.

Nate didn't say anything but merely got into bed. He lay still, alone again with his thoughts. *I might as well be a prisoner,* he thought to himself. *I can't escape these awful thoughts. My future, or what was once my future, is now just a blank page. All I ever wanted to do was fly.*

After tossing and turning for a while, Nate sat up and reached under his bunk for his bag. Out of it he pulled his constant companion—his diary. If he couldn't talk out loud to someone—and he didn't really want to—the next best thing was to write down what he was feeling. Pen in hand, Nate wrote, "Disappointment—lessons—resolutions—new horizons. May His will be done."[1]

On Saturday morning Nate received the bittersweet news. Out of eighty men, he had been chosen as one of nine to become cadets. As he was receiving the back-slapping congratulations, Nate said little. Ignoring the "What's wrong with him?" looks from his buddies, he quietly slipped away to see the "doc." The exam made official his worst fears: He would never fly for the army. Instead of "Accepted limited service," his army card would now be stamped "Disqualified for combat crew duty." Nate was also ordered to the army hospital in Sioux City until his condition improved.

On August 31, the day after his twentieth birthday, Nate wrote to his mother. He had had time to think some more, and his thoughts now returned, typically, to God's Word.

> *I've spent three days loafing and getting used to the new perspective. After a month of tense concentration on winged hopes, an eclipse of those hopes left*

me in a sort of daze. . .I'm not forgetting, 'Boast not thyself of tomorrow; for thou knowest not what a day may bring forth,' but I think the Lord wants us to pray and plan to the very best of our ability, using what He has given us, even if He has to reverse those plans.[2]

Once released from the hospital, Nate spent another month at Morningside College before he hopped on the army "bus" to new destinations. After a three-month stint at Amarillo Field in Texas, Nate was assigned to Baer Field in Fort Wayne, Indiana. He would spend the next eighteen months there, working toward a new goal. If he couldn't be a pilot, he could become an airplane mechanic and receive his "E" license (for engine mechanic). Before he left Amarillo, he wrote a letter to a friend, describing his new state of mind.

The Lord has given me plenty of time to see things differently from the view I had when I went to the hospital. . . . He has taught me a lot about patience. . . . He's a wonderful Teacher—patient and forgiving.

They have made up special orders for me to proceed to Fort Wayne, Indiana. If flying is 'out,' I want to be useful in some way. It will feel good to get greasy, get a few calluses, skin my knuckles on a gadget, hurry to get 'er ready to go on time, and go to bed really tired again.[3]

That was the way he liked to live because that was the way he had been raised.

TWO

From his artistic father, Nate had likely inherited the love of getting "greasy," and from his mother's side had come the urge to "skin his knuckles on a gadget." The tow-haired, blue-eyed boy named Nathanael, but called a variety of nicknames, was born August 30, 1923, into an unusual and robust family that sprawled all over a farmhouse in Huntingdon Valley, Pennsylvania. There was always a pot of soup simmering on the kitchen stove and interesting conversation percolating in many rooms.

Nate was the seventh of eight children born to Lawrence and Katherine Proctor Saint. While Lawrence enjoyed a distinguished career as a designer of stained-glass windows, and Katherine, the daughter of a successful inventor, took care of the house and children, the couple's foremost concern was maintaining a Christian home. Nate's parents had met at a gospel mission in nearby Philadelphia, and their love of the Lord was passed on in generous doses to their children, who were all named after Bible figures. There were rules—no alcohol, tobacco, dancing, going to movies, or gambling—but there was also a love of Scripture and a keen appreciation of God's world outside. Sundays, when the Sabbath was strictly observed in the Saint home, were spent having picnics and going hiking as well as sitting in a church pew. In the winter there was sledding and skating to be enjoyed, and in summer, fishing, swimming, and swinging wildly on a rope swing. Lawrence, who spent long hours most days in his artist's studio, once unveiled a homemade roller coaster, made entirely by him for his energetic brood, that was a miniature version of those found in amusement parks.

Rachel, nine years older than Nate, quickly assumed the care and nurturing of her beautiful little brother. The only girl among seven boys, she saw in Nate a sensitive nature and loving spirit. She liked nothing better than to read stories of missionaries to him, and he usually sat enthralled. "Maybe someday you can go to China like Hudson Taylor," she said one day after finishing a particularly rousing story. "Or to deepest Africa like David Livingstone!"

Nate nodded his head eagerly. He liked missionary stories because they were about people who wanted everyone to be nice to each other. Soon he told Rachel that he was a Christian, too. But several years would pass before he confessed his faith in front of others.

When he was older, Nate wanted to spend more time with his brother Sam, who already had earned his pilot's license. At ten years old, after a few years of being strictly a passenger in the plane, Nate was allowed to take the controls of Sam's plane for the first time. Sam was patient with his young admirer and pupil, instructing him carefully and taking over when Nate became anxious. When Sam held the controls, Nate looked up at the never-ending expanse of blue sky. He didn't want to be in a classroom or studio or office the rest of his life. He wanted to be flying!

After that flight, Nate told his mother that was what he wanted to do—be a pilot like Sam. God had given him this dream, and he had to run with it.

His spiritual wings would come first, though, during Nate's thirteenth summer when he attended a Christian camp in the Poconos. After he had made a public declaration of faith one Saturday evening at the camp, he returned home with renewed Christian vigor. In the fall of 1936, Nate gave a talk to the young people of his church, speaking from notes he had scribbled on notebook paper (later saved by his mother). Among the "points" made were the following:

1. Paul said in Acts, "Believe on the Lord Jesus
   Christ, and thou shalt be saved, and thy house."
   I believe, therefore I am saved and heaven-bound.

   Being saved, I have a purpose because Jesus
   said, "Go ye into all the world and preach the
   gospel to every creature."[1]

Nate closed his talk by quoting the apostle Paul: "I have fought a good fight, I have finished my course, I have kept the faith: Henceforth there is laid up for me a crown of righteousness, which the Lord, the righteous judge, shall give me at that day: and not to me only, but unto all them also that love his appearing."

A year later, he would depend on his faith in God to keep his pilot's dream alive. At age fourteen Nate was diagnosed with osteomyelitis in his right leg, an infection that would keep him at home for months. Without penicillin, the infection had to heal on its own, and at times the pain was excruciating. One night when the pain was particularly intense, Nate prayed more fervently than usual. "Please,

God, if it be Your will, please let me live. If You do, I promise to serve You forever. I'm giving You my life, God, to use any way You want."

God answered his prayer by healing his leg so well that he walked without limping, and Nate soon returned to his activities at church and school. Now, though, the dream of flying began to intrude on his waking thoughts more and more. He couldn't stand being cooped up in a classroom all those hours when he had better things to do. When he was a senior in high school, he got permission from his parents to drop out and take a daytime job in a machinist's shop. Meanwhile, he attended night school in Philadelphia, finishing his degree in a couple of months. In the early summer of 1941, a month or so shy of eighteen, Nate took his first certified flying lesson. At the time, he was working at an airfield outside Philadelphia, just to be close to planes. After the flying lesson, though, Nate used his hard-earned money to buy a small plane that he could tinker with. Determined and driven, Nate wanted to know as much about planes, inside and out, that he could. In a few months, he was even able to sell the plane at a profit.

Nate's knowledge of flying was given a boost when Sam Saint, then a captain with American Airlines, got his little brother a job at LaGuardia Airport as an apprentice mechanic. For a year Nate would live with his brother and his new family, saving every penny to buy his own mechanic's tools. From there, because he soon tired of the rat race of New York, he decided to enter the army.

On New Year's Eve 1944, Nate found himself in Detroit, Michigan. Although the army had sent him from Baer Field to a Ford Motor plant in Detroit to study airplane engines, Nate was to discover another calling after a church service. He hadn't been listening to the pastor's sermon that evening.

Instead, he was carrying on his own conversation with God. He was craving peace—peace that his life was somehow going in the right direction or peace that God would show him a new way. In a letter to a friend, Nate described what happened.

> As soon as I could, I stepped out of that building [the church]. . . . It was snowing and there was already a deep virgin snow on the ground, and the moan of city traffic was muffled. . . . A joy, such as I had never known since the night I accepted Jesus' forgiveness for my sins, seemed to leave me almost weak with gratitude. I was completely relaxed and happy again. The verse that fitted itself to my thoughts was the one that says, "And they found the man. . .sitting. . . clothed, and in his right mind." The old life of chasing things that are of a temporal sort seemed absolutely insane, once the Lord had shown me the new plan.[2]

To Nate, the "new plan" was unmistakably the mission field. Indeed, it took an act of God to persuade a young man who had lived and breathed the nuts and bolts of flying since the age of seven that his life's purpose might be elsewhere. In his next letter to his mother and sister, Nate wrote, "I've always believed that if the Lord wants a guy in full-time service on the mission field, He would make him unbearably miserable in the pursuit of any other end. So, methinks the aircraft industry has suffered the loss of a 'big operator' and the Lord has won for Himself a 'li'l operator.'"[3]

With a new year and a new plan and a new commitment, Nate was ready for the next step. Where in all the world did God want to send him, and what would He do with him when he got there?

THREE

Not everyone in Nate's family knew of his decision to go to the mission field. When an article in *The Sunday School Times* caught Lawrence Saint's eye, he immediately thought of his son Nate. After all, Nate *was* a pilot *and* a mechanic *and* a Christian. Maybe, his father surmised, this was something his son should consider. The article was written by James C. Truxton, who was identified as the president of the newly formed Christian Airmen's Missionary Fellowship (CAMF).

Truxton was one of three World War II pilots who had been meeting for a couple of years to pray and study the Bible—and to discuss the possibility of missionary aviation. Before the war ended, he wanted to establish an organization that could serve missionaries in remote areas. In the article, he was inviting interested Christian pilots to contact him at the CAMF office in Los Angeles.

Nate read the article his father had sent with interest but also a twinge of dismay. Now that he had made the commitment to go to the mission field, he didn't want to be just a mechanic in some lonely hangar somewhere in South

America! He wanted to be out there preaching, teaching, and doing, like the missionaries he remembered from Rachel's storybook. Still, he couldn't ignore the pull on his heart that he had felt after reading Truxton's plea. On January 15, 1945, Nate wrote back from Baer Field.

> *Last New Year's Eve in a watch-night service I responded to the missionary challenge. Have been interested in missionary work for some time, but the Lord owned only my finances. He now has my life.*
>
> *I'm not making any air castle assumptions but want to further the cause of Christ in any way I can, so please count me in and keep me informed of the goings on.[1]*

He would keep in touch with CAMF, but he was still obligated to the army for one more year. During that time, he was not to remain in one place too long. In June he was shipped to Salinas, California, and from there to Merced. He hoped this was his final move, because he kept an ongoing correspondence with many people and hated to keep changing addresses. Among his female correspondents was the daughter of a woman he had met while attending church in Michigan.

Joanna Montgomery was now in nurses' training at California Lutheran Hospital in Los Angeles. She had shared Nate's often humorous letters—and a recent snapshot—with a classmate, not realizing the effect they would have. Now Marj Farris couldn't stop thinking about this man she had never met. Somehow he seemed like the kind of Christian man she wanted to marry. She knew he was stationed in California, so there was always the chance they could meet, even if that seemed unlikely.

Just before Thanksgiving, as she was walking into the lounge of the nurses' residence, Marj saw Joanna talking to a blond soldier in uniform. *It has to be him,* she thought wildly, trying quickly to compose herself. As she pushed back her light brown curls, she chided herself for not losing those few extra pounds. He was just the way she had pictured him, only taller. He was laughing at one of his own jokes, way before the punch line.

After they were introduced, Nate talked to both Marj and Joanna for a while. Hours later, in the privacy of her room, Marj told Joanna that Nate was the man she wanted to marry.

Nate, who left without making further plans to see Marj, was taken with her, as well. He was interested in meeting someone who could be his life's mate, as he had confided to his father at about this same time. "Suffice to say that I, too, am interested in your future daughter-in-law—but I doubt whether the Lord has yet shown me His treasure."[2]

But after meeting Marj, Nate wrote in his diary, "I was immediately captivated, but tried to hold the fort because I had no idea who she was. After she left us I asked Jo about her—and walked all the way up to the center of town kicking myself every step, the way you would if you had just thrown away a winning ticket, then found it was the winning number."[3]

Romance would have to wait for Nate, despite his attraction to the pretty Marj Farris. After he was honorably discharged from the army in February 1946, he returned home to Huntingdon Valley to kill a few months. Since God had called him to the mission field on that snowy New Year's Eve in Detroit, Nate had given his future a great deal of thought. Before he went anywhere as a missionary, he needed more education, at least a couple years of college. To enroll, however, he had to wait until the end of the semester, sometime in May or June. He was considering applying to Westmont College in Santa Barbara, California, which would also put him many miles closer to Los Angeles, but he was also interested in Wheaton College, the well-known Christian training ground outside Chicago from which so many pastors and missionaries had graduated.

While he was leafing through applications, CAMF was preparing to launch its first plane service. Nate had been in touch with Betty Greene, CAMF's first pilot, and she had described the mission to him. CAMF was to begin by flying supplies and personnel from Tuxtla Gutierrez, Mexico, one hundred miles inland to the Wycliffe Bible Translators' jungle camp, which would be serviced by an airstrip at El Real. Nate could picture the plane very well—a 1933 red Waco biplane that had a new 220-horsepower engine. Betty, an experienced pilot, was leaving for Peru after making this inaugural run. There she would anchor another CAMF operation. She would be flying to El Real with her "successor" on board, another seasoned pilot named George Wiggins.

But the next news Nate received wasn't what he expected or wanted to hear. The flight had gone well until Betty was preparing to land at El Real. Somehow the plane had clipped a small building, causing severe damage to the aircraft. They had been forced to abandon the plane on the runway, since neither Betty nor George was an airplane mechanic. Jim Truxton, writing to Nate, asked him to come to Mexico right away, all expenses covered.

Nate was undecided. Going to Mexico would mean postponing college for at least another semester, if he knew anything about airplane repair. But not going would mean not giving a helping hand to an organization that was literally trying to get off the ground. After praying about the matter, Nate wrote back that he could be there in a couple of weeks.

Two days later, train tickets arrived from California. Nate was to leave from Philadelphia almost immediately. Saying good-bye to his baffled parents, Nate headed west. *If this is what God meant by the mission field,* he thought, *well, I'm going without looking back, and without too much thought for my journey.*

At the Texas-Mexico border, Nate was instructed by CAMF to ship the new propeller by train to Tuxtla. (He would fly to Mexico City and from there to Tuxtla.) Just getting to Tuxtla, the capital of Chiapas, was an adventure for Nate, whose travel experience so far had been limited to going to and from army bases. If he could survive the sweltering heat of St. Louis as he ran to make his connecting train, and if he could be agile enough to hang on by a finger to the back of a Mexican bus, he could handle himself in the sleepy town of Tuxtla.

Despite his less-than-luxurious accommodations that he sometimes shared with a mule and pig, Nate was most dismayed by what he found at the local airport. There were the panels of the damaged wings in a basket, with pieces of the rest of the plane thrown haphazardly in a corner of a hangar. One thing he knew for sure: He couldn't do this job alone. An "E" license did not mean he could build an entire airplane from scratch.

With the help of a Mexican cabinetmaker and further assistance from a Wycliffe translator named Phil Baer, Nate made slow but steady progress on the repairs. News of the outside world, as well as monthly missionary paychecks, came from Charles Mellis, who was serving as secretary of CAMF. To Charles, Nate described the food: "Chow tonight was black beans, or frijoles, two hard-boiled eggs, coffee, rolls, and (let me never forget) tortillas. A tortilla looks like it should line a saddle."[4] He also described in less humorous fashion the "malarial climate" and his own bout with a form of Montezuma's revenge. Nate was also bedridden for a time with jaundice.

Finally, Nate and Phil were ready to fly to El Real. After chartering a plane and loading it with the repaired parts, they took off for the infamous airstrip where the rest of the plane was still moored. As expected, Nate found the plane a disaster, except, providentially, for the engine. Trouble was, Nate now had only a week left on his six-month work permit to complete the job. Working night and day, Nate used bedsheets to patch the fuselage and attached the wings in the middle of a rainstorm.

Although he tried to talk George Wiggins out of flying the patched-together aircraft—"I wanted him to understand that I believed the plane was safe enough for a single fellow with no dependents but not for a man with a family"[5]—George soared away by himself, leaving Nate to return to the United States.

Without going to college, Nate had already figuratively compiled a textbook on missionary life. Nonetheless, he was pleased when he returned home to find an acceptance letter waiting for him from Wheaton College. His first classes would begin in January 1947. Unlike the old Nate, he couldn't wait to get back in the classroom.

FOUR

Nate could be a model student for only so long. After throwing himself into his classwork at Wheaton and receiving high marks, he started to long for that big expanse of blue sky. By spring he found a part-time job at a local airport, and he could also be spotted doing street evangelism work in downtown Chicago. He was going to bed tired again.

He was also keeping in touch with his old friends at CAMF, which since the previous September was now called the Missionary Aviation Fellowship (MAF). Since their launch in Mexico, the fledgling group had experienced some bumpy moments. Two crashes, one in Mexico and one in Ecuador, had not resulted in any fatalities, but the safety of the aircraft was in question, not to mention the future of the operation. To discuss the situation in more detail, Nate made plans to meet Charlie Mellis in June when both would be attending a missionary convention in New York.

At a coffee shop near the convention center, both men settled comfortably onto the vinyl benches. Charlie couldn't help but smile when looking at Nate's laughing face. His blue eyes twinkled constantly, but they also revealed a keen mind that was always at work. Already Nate had shared some improvements MAF might make on the aircraft, and he was especially interested in improving the efficiency of the operation in dense jungle areas.

Then Charlie tapped the table gently with his knuckles. "I almost forgot, Nate. You'll never guess who I ran into the other day. Marj Farris."

At the mention of her name, Nate fixed his gaze on his coffee cup. When Charlie didn't say anything, Nate looked up. "And?"

Charlie laughed at his friend's obvious curiosity. "Thought you might be interested. Actually, didn't talk to her much, but it's what I saw. She was with another guy. Looks like they're dating."

The subject then changed back to airplanes, even though Nate's heart was elsewhere. The first thing he would do when he got back to Pennsylvania was write Joanna's mother. She would know what was going on with Marj and whether he should write her or just move on.

In the weeks that followed, with Mrs. Montgomery acting as matchmaker, Nate and Marj started corresponding by letter. But Nate wanted more than just letters once Mrs. Montgomery had assured him that Marj was not dating anyone seriously. Packing his old Ford, he drove to Wheaton College. From there, he hitchhiked to California. He had to see Marj in person.

This time when they saw each other, all the other barriers melted away. Nate was no longer a stranger and no longer a soldier with an obligation to the military. Marj, who had finished her nurses' training, was no longer insecure about where she stood with Nate. Love soon blossomed, with their feelings growing stronger with each passing day. After he left California, Nate wrote Marj, "The fog is thinning out and my heart tells me the story. . . . I love you. My heart has been singing that song all along but my head was off pitch for awhile. I know now that it is love. . .the realest, deepest kind a fellow can know."[1]

Nate returned to Wheaton in the fall, but he was already thinking about Christmas. He and Marj had made plans to meet at her home in Idaho, where he would be introduced to her parents for the first time. But his academic life was also interrupted by his ongoing correspondence with Charlie Mellis. Before Christmas break, Charlie asked Nate to pray about going into the mission field sooner rather than later. Charlie and Jim Truxton had a specific place in mind for someone with Nate's mechanical skills, a place, as Charlie described, that had just two landing areas—"the top of the jungle or the raging rapids of a river." The place was Ecuador.

That Christmas in Idaho, Nate and Marj became engaged. Over her parents' objection, Marj followed Nate back to Wheaton College, where she enrolled in a few classes while working at a nearby hospital. When they were together, the couple prayed and talked about their future in the mission field. Nate had also been considering the possibility of going to New Guinea, but a visit in early February from Charlie Mellis changed his mind. The couple decided to get married earlier than they had planned and go back to California to attend the Bible Institute of Los Angeles for a semester. From there, they would leave for Ecuador.

"Perhaps I've gotten into the habit of barging in where angels fear to tread," Nate wrote at that time, "but I still have the ability to say 'sorry' if it becomes evident that the job is too tough. We know if we humbly seek His face in the matter, crucifying our own desires, we can't go wrong. . . . Fear and faith are not fellow travelers."[2]

On Valentine's Day 1948, Marj and Nate were married in his brother Sam's church on Long Island. To Nate, they would now be fellow travelers, but more important, they would be partners in spreading the gospel. Marj only had to look inside her wedding ring to know her husband's heart. Turning the band to catch the light, she read, "O magnify the Lord with me, and let us exalt his name together" (Psalm 34:3).

FIVE

Nothing but green below, he thought. Dense, impenetrable green. Nate, sitting in the relatively unfamiliar passenger seat of the MAF plane, couldn't take his eyes away from the lush rain forests of the Oriente, as the eastern jungle of Ecuador was called. He and Jim Truxton were on the final leg of a journey that had begun in Brownsville, Texas, on September 8, 1948. After refueling in Ecuador's capital city of Quito, they were on their way, at last, to Shell Mera, MAF's base of operation on the edge of the jungle.

"We're just about there, Nate. Look, there's the clearing!" Jim shouted to Nate above the noise of the engine.

"Civilization!" Nate yelled back. Down below were actual roads and buildings and multiple landing strips. From his many briefings with Jim and the MAF, Nate knew the history of the area by heart. Shell Mera—named after the town of Mera several miles away—was the Shell Oil Company headquarters, which had been established ten years earlier. No expense had been spared to construct the facility so that Shell would have the opportunity to explore the Oriente for possible oil reserves.

Once Jim had expertly landed the remodeled Stinson craft, Nate jumped out, eager to examine his new surroundings. There, across from the landing strip, was the piece of land that would become Nate's home. The only thing missing was the house itself, and that couldn't happen too soon. Heavy on his heart was the absence of his partner, best friend, and soon-to-be mother of his first child. Marj and Jim's wife had flown by commercial airplane to Quito, where they would be staying until the house at Shell Mera was completed. Their baby was due in early January. As soon as Marj was here, Nate thought, their mission could really begin.

"Let's set up camp, Nate," Jim called to him. They had brought tents and camping supplies so they could rough it until the house took shape.

That night, sitting out looking up at the stars, Nate knew he was where God had called him to be. From a snowy night in Detroit to a brilliant, spangled evening in Shell Mera, he had tried to follow God's leading. Only God could have brought him to a place where he would be doing what he loved so that others would be able to find the peace and joy that seemed to burst from his pores. Now that he was here, he wanted to throw himself into the life of the jungle. He wanted to get to know, as he wrote earlier to friends, "the vast dank dungeon of the mighty Amazon where thousands are bound in darkness by chains of sin."[1]

Nate loved the mornings when he had a better view, as he said, of God's creative handiwork. When the sun climbed high in the sky, he and Jim could see the snow-covered peak of Sangay, an active volcano less than fifty miles away. Besides the star show at night, the two men were often treated to Sangay's fiery display, with red shooting streams arching into the black sky. Jim also pointed out the snow-covered crater in the distance to the west known as El Altar.

Then there were the many tropical flowers, set against a backdrop of green. Taking a break from their work one day, Nate and Jim came across lavender orchids growing by the side of the main road that had been built by Shell and led to Ambato. Sometimes living at the end of what he thought of as civilization, it was difficult for Nate to believe there was another Ecuador out there, too. But nothing less than a thorough education of his new home would satisfy MAF's newest recruit.

Straddling the equator, Ecuador is one of the smallest countries in South America but among the most diverse geographically. Besides the Oriente, which covers one-half of the country, there are the Costa, or coastal plain, and the Sierra, or central highlands, the two most populated regions, and the Galapagos Islands, which contain many extinct volcanoes, as well as plant and animal species.

Although Nate hadn't met many natives yet, he knew most Ecuadoreans were of Indian descent, with Spanish as the official language. Out here in the Oriente, however, the language spoken was Quichua, which was also the name of the largest group of Indian peoples. After the Quichua, the Jivaro were most populous, a tribe best known for its skill at shrinking and preserving the heads of their victims. And, while Ecuador was considered a Roman Catholic country, in the Oriente the Indian peoples maintained their ancient religions, religions often based on superstition and vengeance.

Despite Shell Mera's idyllic setting, Nate could feel an undercurrent of paganism in the jungle. That was why he was there.

Within days the number of tents had increased, thanks to

the willing hands of other missionaries in the area. Charlie Mellis's father, who was a retired builder, had even come all the way from St. Louis just to supervise the construction. With all the activity going on, Nate was soon freed up to start making airborne deliveries to other jungle stations. Working among the Quichua Indians in the towns of Pano, Dos Rios, and Ahjuana were Henry Miller, David Cooper, and Morris Fuller and their families. Those who served the Jivaro were Frank Drown and Keith Austin in Macuma and Mike Ficke in Sucua. Another Jivaro camp at Chupientsa was without an airstrip and had to be reached by mules.

Nate was welcomed wildly wherever he went because the need was so great. "Did you know Macuma has been without fresh food and medicine for five months?" he exclaimed to Jim one evening. "And today I was able to bring home David Cooper's wife—a journey that normally would have taken three days by foot!"

Jim smiled and nodded. "Now you know why I've been praying for you to come. And you've only just started. Wait until you see what God can do here, Nate. When the house is finished and Marj is here—can you begin to see?"

By October, the house was ready and Marj made plans to fly from Quito to Ambato, where Nate would meet her to fly home to Shell Mera. The house, which they dubbed "Shell Merita," was designed for the jungle climate. Constructed of lumber from native trees that had been stained brown, it boasted a corrugated aluminum roof that was positioned several inches above the house to allow for airflow inside. Inside was a large room that served as living room, dining room, and radio room, a kitchen, and just outside, a meat closet to store smoked meats. From the kitchen window one could see the landing strip and the small airplane hangar, as well as breathtaking views of the mountains and nearby jungle.

In the few months before she had to leave again for Quito to have the baby, Marj became most familiar with the radio operation. She would be Nate's sole contact at Shell Mera when he was flying, as well as the radio contact to the other missionary stations. (Before she knew it, she would be called "Mom Saint" because of her key role in shepherding supplies and taking such loving care of all her "charges.") Thrilled to be back together with her husband, the two of them often talked about their goals as missionaries.

In a letter written to Charlie Mellis, Nate summed up his and Marj's desires. "The Indian is the motive," he wrote. "But all I know about him is that he's lost unless I keep the airplane going and get the news to him."[2] In his few quiet moments when he found himself thinking more and more about his native neighbors, who had little or no knowledge of salvation, he could feel his heart beat a little faster. And when he talked with other missionaries, his interest was piqued all the more. It was then that he learned one of the most feared names in the Oriente—the *Auca*.

Sitting around the campfire, David Cooper spoke in almost hushed tones about the legendary tribe. "They're known as the naked Aucas because that's how they don't dress, but they're better known as savages. The Quichua even named them *Auca,* a word that means 'savage.' We haven't gotten close enough to know their real name. I've tried to reach them in small ways, and so has Dr. Tidmarsh [a Plymouth Brethren missionary]. For three centuries no one has been allowed to get to know them—except, of course, by reputation."

"Three centuries!" Nate whistled through his teeth. "But what do they do exactly?"

"They prefer to ambush their victims, then pierce them with nine-foot spears—exactly."

"What caused them to be so hostile? From what I've

heard, the Quichua aren't like that, and the Jivaro are hostile only with certain tribes."

Cooper proceeded to relate what he knew. Reports of deaths by hostile Indian attacks went back to the mid-sixteenth century when Gonzalo Pizarro sent one of his lieutenants to explore the Amazon region. While many men died of tropical illnesses, many were killed by supposed ancestors of the Aucas, as were many Jesuit missionaries who followed the Spanish explorers in the next century. When rubber hunters entered the Amazon region in the middle of the nineteenth century, a different scene played out. Young male Auca Indians were lured away from their villages by the hunters with promises of gifts, only to realize later that they had been tricked into becoming slaves at Spanish haciendas. Their villages were subsequently ravaged and many of the women and children killed. Years of enduring such cruelty were most likely responsible for the ferocity of the Aucas.

When Shell Oil Company arrived on the edge of the Oriente and proceeded to blast away roads and campsites, the Aucas attacked again. In 1942, three employees of Shell were killed at Arajuno, the closest campsite to Auca territory. One year later eight more employees were brutally murdered.

"There is an Auca girl named Dayuma who escaped from the tribe when her parents were murdered in an intertribal dispute," Cooper said. "She's living with the Quichuas now and has changed her appearance so she looks like a Quichua woman."

"What does she say about the Aucas?" Nate asked quietly. "Have you found out anything that might be useful in reaching them?"

Dave shook his head. "Not much. In fact, the news is

pretty dismal. Whenever Dayuma is asked why the Aucas kill, she says it's because they're killers. Over and over she has said, 'Never, never trust them.'"

Days later, Nate wrote to his parents about the Aucas. "Not long ago we talked to another missionary who is longing to contact a tribe of killers. Neighboring tribes live in mortal fear of them. We expect the airplane will somehow play an essential part in the reaching of these people one day with the gospel.

"We're watching and praying for that day."[3]

SIX

By year's end, Nate's plans to reach an unreached tribe were tabled indefinitely. Instead of flying over the rain forests of the Oriente, Nate found himself in a hospital bed in Quito. He had crashed the Stinson through no fault of his own, and now the entire MAF operation in Ecuador was on hold.

Since the beginning of December, on doctor's orders, Marj had been staying in Quito, awaiting the birth of her baby. Following a weekend visit with her, Nate was planning to fly back to Shell Mera with a missionary's wife and her son. But when the plane became airborne, wily air currents sent the craft hurtling toward the ground, with Nate doing his best to land in some fashion. There were no casualties. Mrs. Tidmarsh suffered cuts and a few broken bones, and her son Robert had minor injuries, but Nate would be out of commission for a while. When he awoke in the recovery room of the hospital, he was clad in almost a full-body cast.

Nine days later, while Nate was in another hospital in Panama having his back reexamined, Marj gave birth in Quito to a beautiful girl. Kathy Joan Saint would soon become the pride of Shell Merita. There would be an empty hangar, but the house would be filled with joy. The hangar wouldn't be empty for long, though. Another plane and another pilot had been secured by MAF, the pilot only temporary until Nate got out of his cast.

Needless to say, the crash at Quito had started the wheels turning in Nate's active brain. He didn't have the power to prevent air currents, but he now had the time to implement some safety devices he had been considering. Watching a young Indian boy ride on top of a truck funneling gasoline to another boy sitting on the front fender, his arm inside the hood, gave Nate his first idea. For some time he had been concerned about the safety of a single-engine plane stopping in mid-air over the jungle. If he could devise an alternate fuel system, the plane would be much safer. The next day, Nate began experiments that would eventually lead to a four-pound rig that fit the bill, eventually winning approval from the Civil Aeronautics Authority.

That accomplished, Nate turned his attention to the problem of delivering goods to missionaries stationed in areas where no airstrip could be built. Setting his mind in motion was a scene from his Wheaton College days, being in a stuffy classroom, watching a pencil swinging from a string. With a canvas bucket and fifteen hundred feet of cord, one end tied to the bucket and the other fastened to the plane, Nate began experimenting with a bucket-drop system. By turning the plane sharply with the bucket dangling behind, he discovered the bucket would then begin to spiral slowly toward earth. When he lifted the plane, the bucket came up, too. As soon as he was able to begin flying again, Nate discovered many uses for the bucket drop. Not only could he deliver mail, supplies, and medicine this way, but he could also send down an aerial telephone so he and the missionaries could deliver messages to each other.

That accomplished, the weight of the plane became Nate's next concern. He was thinking of all the supplies and people that he would be ferrying from one place to the next. It made no sense for a jungle plane to carry unnecessary weight when there was so much that had to be on board. After replacing the eight-pound seats with one-pound substitutes, he looked around the outside of the plane and removed the fenders on the wheels of the plane. These often became caked with mud, weighing down the aircraft.

Naturally, Nate compared these changes to spiritual matters. Writing to MAF headquarters, he said:

> When life's flight is over, and we unload our cargo at the other end, the fellow who got rid of unnecessary weight will have the most valuable cargo to present to the Lord. Not only that. There's another secret. Two air-planes may look alike, but one may be able to lift twice the load into the air. The difference is the horsepower of the engine. Bible reading is the power of the Christian life. Dead weight doesn't do you any good and a big plane with little horsepower doesn't go anywhere.[1]

Once Nate was back in the pilot's seat, making as many as fifteen flights a day, he began to make plans to improve Shell Merita. By the time the Saints returned to the United States in February 1952 for their first furlough, many changes had taken place.

The homestead was now equipped with hydroelectric power, thanks to Nate's plan to dam the stream at the rear of the MAF property. That was necessary to operate the short-wave radio that became Marj's constant companion, as well as other household appliances. And because Shell Merita was the base of MAF's operation in Ecuador, missionaries on their way in or out of the jungle, as well as mission executives, often spent the night as guests of Marj and Nate. Plans were put into motion to expand the house to accommodate twenty or more guests, as well as install the first shower bath (done by Nate).

More guests were expected when Shell Oil decided to terminate its operation at Shell Mera in 1949. Thanks to good terms accepted by Shell, the Gospel Missionary Union (GMU) was able to purchase land and several buildings that had once belonged to the oil company to establish a permanent Bible school. The Berean Bible Institute would be under the direction of Keith and Doris Austin, who had been missionaries at Macuma. For themselves personally, Marj and Nate were able to purchase a kerosene stove and a hot-water tank from Shell, making their lives easier and more pleasant. Since the birth of their second child, Stephen Farris Saint, in January 1951, the smooth running of the household was a top priority.

In the mission field, Nate and Marj had exciting news to report to the churches that supported them back home. Before they left for furlough, an airstrip had opened at Chupientsa, the formerly unreachable mission to the Jivaros served faithfully for many years by George Moffat and his wife. Nate and Marj had once visited Chupientsa by mule, a trip that had taken more than six hours from Shell Mera over backbreaking trails. Having an airstrip would make an incredible difference in the lives of the Moffats.

Before Nate handed over the "reins" to another MAF couple who would handle the flying and the radio operation at Shell Merita, he was able to play host to his sister, Rachel. Taking her out for a flight over the rain forest, Nate pointed out the many villages he served and what missionaries were serving where. As they circled over the deserted camp of Arajuno, Rachel seemed puzzled. She strained her eyes to see something, anything, that signaled the presence of human life.

"What's down there? It doesn't look like anyone lives there."

Nate laughed. "That's what the Aucas would like you to think. You're looking at the next adventure, sis, just over that ridge."

By the end of 1953, new missionaries had arrived in the Oriente. Frank and Marie Drown were still at Macuma, thirty-five minutes (flying time) southeast from Shell Mera, serving the Jivaro, but they had been joined by GMU missionaries Roger and Barbara Youderian. Plymouth Brethren missionaries Jim and Elisabeth (Betty) Elliot were in Puyupungu, seven minutes southeast of Shell Mera, and Ed and Marilou McCully were at Shandia, along with Pete Fleming, twenty minutes northeast of Nate's home base.

Where there had been only twelve missionaries in the region in 1948 when Nate and Marj arrived, by 1954 there were twenty-five. Nate rejoiced when MAF, recognizing the burgeoning need, sent another pilot to help run the routes. In the spring of 1955, Johnny Keenan arrived with his family and immediately became Nate's right-hand man. Marj, though, was busier than ever with the arrival of Philip Jonathan in December and her increasing responsibilities as radio contact. Often, she balanced Philip on her hip while speaking into the microphone to a needy missionary.

By the fall of 1955, Pete and Olive Fleming, who were newlyweds, took over the Puyupungu station, and Jim and Betty moved to Shandia, serving the Quichuas. Since the summer of 1954, Roger and Barbara had been at Wambimi, still farther south of Macuma, serving the Atshuaras, the Jivaros' deadly enemy and an unreached people. Meanwhile, the McCullys moved to Arajuno, the deserted Shell camp on the edge of Auca territory, where they were working with another colony of Quichuas and hoping for a chance to contact the Aucas.

Roger, Jim, Ed, and Pete were as committed as Nate to the mission field, as the "old hand" pilot soon discovered. At one time or another, all of them had visited Shell Mera—some for instruction in Spanish at the Bible institute, some even to give birth to their children—and Nate had flown supplies to them or ferried them and their wives on a regular basis. Nate appreciated that they were different men, from different backgrounds, joined in the Oriente for a common purpose: to reach the unreached.

Roger Youderian was from Montana, a decorated soldier who had survived the Battle of the Bulge despite having suffered from polio as a child. Jim Elliot, an Oregonian and Wheaton College graduate, was a champion wrestler in college. Ed McCully, who knew Jim at Wheaton and hailed from Wisconsin, was a stellar athlete as well as a prize-winning orator who had left law school to pursue the mission field. Finally, Pete Fleming, from the state of Washington, had received a master's degree in literature and was expected to become a college professor until God's call changed his course.

Until September 19, 1955, Nate had no thought that his mission goal and that of these fellow laborers for Christ would be exactly the same, that they would live and breathe the name *Auca* for the next three and a half months. He had no thought that for decades or longer to come, from pulpits, classrooms, and in magazines and books, his name and theirs would be mentioned, almost always, in the same sentence.

SEVEN

Nate had flown over Auca territory before. When Ed and Marilou McCully moved into the camp at Arajuno, he had, at Ed's request, made an aerial survey of the area. Like an earlier time when he had shown his sister this same patch of rain forest, Nate noted no signs of life. There was only dense, lush forest threaded with muddy brown rivers—no smoke, no living quarters, no fleeting glimpses of a child playing or a man hunting.

September 19 was the date of one more routine visit to deliver supplies to Arajuno. As usual, Nate hopped out of the yellow plane and shook hands with Ed, then helped him with the packages.

"Perfect day for flying," Nate said in greeting.

"Not the usual haze," Ed agreed.

Rubbing his hands together, Nate broached the subject that had occurred to him just before he landed. "What do you say, once we're finished, we go check out your neighbors?"

Ed's eyes lit up at the suggestion. "Sure thing! Let's go raid Marilou's pantry for a few supplies—just in case."

At around nine in the morning, the two men took off. Following the Nushino River east, one of the main arteries in Auca land, they were able to look six to eight miles on either side, thanks to the increased visibility. When they were fifty miles from Arajuno, Ed thought he saw something. "Looks like manioc was once planted there," he said, pointing below. Nate quickly circled back, and they took another look.

"I don't see much there," Nate said, sneaking a look at the gas gauge. "We don't have much fuel left, but I hate to give up. Let's go a few more miles then head back."

Nate thought he had seen something ahead, but from that great a distance it was hard to tell. As they neared Nate's mystery spot, Ed began pointing wildly. "A clearing, Nate! And there's cleaned manioc lying there, too. Go slowly, maybe there's more."

Nate could feel his pulse racing as he spied one clearing after another—maybe fifteen altogether—and even a few houses. It wasn't a good look, but it was definitely what they had wanted to see. Checking the fuel gauge again, Nate signaled to Ed that they had to return to Arajuno. Besides, Nate thought, they didn't want to scare off any Aucas who might have seen them overhead.

Ten days later, on September 29, Nate was scheduled to ferry Jim and Pete and Indian guides to the village of Villano, where they would spend several days. The route would take them over Auca territory, and, best of all to Nate, it would require two trips to ferry all their equipment and supplies. That meant two chances to look for Aucas.

The first trip with Jim and the supplies was uneventful. But on the second, with Pete and the Indian guides, Nate decided to fly farther east than before. Again, the men spotted clearings, a sight that caused the Indian guides to say, without hesitation, "Aucas." They also saw several houses, six larger ones with smaller ones around them.

"Look at your watch, Pete," Nate said. "We're only fifteen minutes from Ed's place. The Aucas are closer than we thought."

The men agreed to keep their findings between themselves, with Pete pressing secrecy upon the guides. A few days later, Jim, Ed, Nate, and Johnny Keenan found themselves poring over a map on the living room floor of Shell Merita. Johnny had gone to pick up Jim at Villano and had run into bad weather, forcing him to come back to home base.

"The Lord is leading us to the Aucas," Jim said. "I feel absolutely convinced that His timing is now."

"But how should we approach them?" Nate asked. "There must be a multitude of ways."

Just peering at the map of the Oriente was numbing, but the men soon became fortified with cups of hot cocoa. As the hands of the clock on the kitchen table crept past midnight, the men came up with the first step of a plan—a plan to be cloaked in secrecy. They did not want to let non-missionary groups know that they were pursuing a savage tribe. There had been talk that some groups were planning an expedition into Auca territory, heavily armed, to retaliate for previous Auca attacks. The missionaries only wanted to make friendly contact for the Lord's sake.

The first step was Jim's idea. Recognizing that they were handicapped because they did not know the Auca language, Jim proposed meeting with Dayuma, the Auca girl who had escaped from her tribe. She was now living on a hacienda that was a four-hour walk from Shandia. Jim was the logical choice to meet with her, since he spoke fluent Quichua, the language Dayuma had adopted. If Dayuma could give him some useful phrases or words, the men might be able to begin their approach to the Aucas.

Less than a week later, Jim returned from his meeting with Dayuma. She had been cooperative, thinking that he was only interested in learning the Auca language, not in meeting with her people. Among the many phrases he had written on note cards were "Biti miti punimupa," which meant "I like you; I want to be your friend," and "Biti winki pungi amupa," which meant "Let's get together."[1]

On October 6 the men decided to implement part two of the plan to reach the Aucas. Nate had been unable to sleep the night before, knowing his expertise was crucial in accomplishing this step. Now that they were armed with a few Auca phrases, they decided to begin making aerial drops over those clearings they had noted earlier. Nate's bucket-drop method—this time dropping a bucket filled with colored buttons, rock salt, and colored ribbons, and then pulling up the line—would be the key to the operation.

After picking up Ed at Arajuno and removing the door on the side of the plane, the two men were airborne over Auca territory. Fifteen minutes later, Nate elbowed Ed. "There's the house we saw before. No people, but it looks like someone's definitely there."

Ed was almost bouncing on his seat. He had missed the trip before when Nate and Pete had spotted what they thought was an Auca village. As Nate slowed the plane, Ed began the well-rehearsed procedure of letting out the line, making sure there were no knots. Then Nate began circling the plane, slowly, until he could see the ribbons from the bucket fluttering below. They had decided to try to land the bucket on the path between the house and the river, since it was likely that Aucas would pass that way several times a day.

After six attempts at lowering, then raising, then lowering again, and one heart-stopping moment when the ribbons became slightly tangled in a tree, the bucket dropped on the ground three feet from the water's edge on a sandbar.

In Nate's diary that night he wrote, "In a sense we had delivered the first gospel-message-by-sign-language to a people who were a quarter of a mile away vertically, fifty miles horizontally, and continents and wide seas away psychologically. How much do these people know? What do they think of what little they have seen of the outside world?"[2]

The men were determined to keep trying. On October 14 Nate and Ed were ready to make a second drop. This time their "gift" was a machete, an invaluable tool in the jungle. First, though, both men were anxious to go back to the site of the first drop to see if the bucket was still there. With his eyes pressed inside binoculars, Ed confirmed it was gone.

"Keep looking, Ed. Here goes the second installment," Nate said, his voice steady and a big smile creasing his face.

As the bucket lowered, streaming behind the plane, Ed yelled out, "I see someone!" Leaving his seat and almost hanging out the door of the plane, Ed craned his neck for a better view. Not just one but several Aucas were running toward the bucket, which was inching steadily closer to the ground. When the bucket finally dropped—in a stream this time—one Auca dived into the water to retrieve it. Several men were waiting on the shore to see the latest gift.

Such "success" emboldened the missionaries to continue. While the third drop eight days later was likely lost in the jungle, the Aucas had been waiting in one of the large clearings, as if expecting the plane to arrive on a regular schedule. Not wanting to lose their momentum, for the fourth drop, the men decided to bring a battery-powered loudspeaker along so they could shout out Auca phrases. This time their gift of another machete, yellow shirt, and beads seemed to be well received.

On the way home Nate followed the path of the Curaray River, hoping to find possible landing sites. His diary entry that night reflected the futile search: "Hopes not good. Guide us, Lord God."[3]

A meeting after this latest drop provided a chance for the men to regroup. While Jim was prepared to make friendly contact as soon as possible with the Aucas and even move his family into their village, Pete felt that not enough preliminary work had been done yet. Ed wanted to continue the search for a possible landing site near the largest collection of houses, a place they had dubbed "Terminal City." Nate, leaning toward a more conservative approach, felt that the aerial drops should continue on a regular basis for a while. On the sixth bucket drop, the wisdom of the pilot would be realized.

On November 12 Ed and Nate headed first for the Curaray, following its path westward. They found one house they had not previously seen and then came upon the site of the first drop. An older man, whose body was smeared with a claylike substance, went out to the sandbar and seemed to be waiting for a gift to drop. Even though the men obliged by dropping another machete, there was little enthusiasm on the face of the recipient.

Nate then flew over the area of one of their later drops and was delighted to see a crowd waiting. Shouting to the people over the public-address system, Ed dropped a small pot out of the plane. When they flew over a larger house where they had previously received another enthusiastic welcome, Nate noticed a field nearby that had recently been cleared—as if for them. When they threw out the line with another pot attached, they could feel the Indians holding onto the line. Looking down, Ed noticed that they had cut off the pot and were attaching something of their own to the line. When the line was reeled in, on the end was tied a headband of woven feathers.

Of that encounter Ed wrote in his diary, "A real answer to prayer; another sign to proceed, an encouragement that friendly relations are possible and that they will hear the gospel!"[4]

By the eighth visit, Nate was becoming more concerned about their number, should they decide on meeting the Aucas face-to-face. There were only four men involved at this point, but Nate had an idea who could be number five. At the time, Roger Youderian was visiting Shell Mera, working on the construction of a hospital by the Bible institute. When Nate approached him about what was now between the men known as "Operation Auca," Roger readily agreed to join. At a crossroads in his missionary life, he longed to reach as many unreached as possible and be truly useful. In short order, Roger gathered his belongings and moved into the base at Arajuno.

On the drop of December 10, the men hurtled down gifts of clothes as well as mounted photographs of each of the men, the photos bearing the symbol of a little yellow plane. Again, the Aucas attached a gift to the end of the line—this time, a parrot in a bark-covered basket, with a partially eaten banana inside! Nate and Ed were pleased with the visit for another reason. This time when cruising the Curaray they had located a beach that might be suitable as a landing strip. Nate had skimmed the wheels on its surface, and the sand seemed firm enough. The beach, which they proceeded to name "Palm Beach," was over four miles away from the Auca settlement.

Once a landing strip had been located, plans began to be made to establish a campsite there, with January 2 as the tentative date of departure. They decided to drop off a prefabricated treehouse and supplies good for two weeks, to be followed by the men on different flights, as well as other supplies. The following day they would take the plane and begin circling the Auca village, inviting the Indians to come to Palm Beach. If no Indians came to the campsite, they were prepared to withdraw by air or down the river in canoes.

Until that time, though, the gift drops continued, with the next to last one on December 23. As Nate and Jim circled the Auca settlement, they saw the same old man they had noticed earlier. When they swooped down to take a closer look, they were concerned by the look on his face. The man looked terrified. After dropping off their gift at another location—this time the bucket contained a flashlight, among other items—they felt the tug on the line as the Aucas attached their gift to them. It was the largest of all the Aucas' gifts, too big even to haul inside the plane. Nate waited until they reached Arajuno to untie the package on the runway. Among the many items were two squirrels, which had been killed by the fall, one live parrot, and a smoked monkey tail.

As Christmas approached, Nate spent much time writing letters to family and friends. While he couldn't discuss Operation Auca openly, he did ask for their prayers. He also penned a letter that could be opened after the operation had been accomplished, addressed to an anonymous "brother in Christ."

> *As we have a high old time this Christmas, may we who know Christ hear the cry of the damned as they hurtle headlong into the Christless night without ever a chance. May we be moved with compassion as our Lord was. May we shed tears of repentance for those whom we have failed to bring out of darkness. Beyond the smiling scenes of Bethlehem may we see the crushing agony of Golgotha. May God give us a new vision of His will concerning the Lost and our responsibility.[4]*

On Monday, January 2, 1956, the missionaries gathered at Arajuno, making final plans for the next day. That night Nate lay awake, his thoughts consumed by his responsibility in the operation and by the brutal acknowledgment that they were actually going into Auca territory. It was a rough decision to go there, he thought. But there was no doubt in his mind that they should continue.

EIGHT

The fog was lifting as Nate's yellow plane approached the Curaray. There had been a few glitches that morning with the plane, but nothing that an emergency trip by Johnny Keenan couldn't handle. That had left the men time to sing a hymn and pray before leaving. At 8:02 A.M. they were airborne, Nate and Ed, on the first trip to Palm Beach. It was Tuesday, January 3, 1956.

As he landed the plane on Palm Beach, Nate felt his heart sink as the wheels dug deep into the soft sand. At least there were two of them, he thought, and he had been able to land without crashing. After depositing Ed and some supplies and repositioning the plane, Nate was able to find some harder sand for the take-off. The situation was helped when Johnny, who was staying at Arajuno to make sure the operation succeeded, suggested letting out some of the air in the tires.

After five trips between Arajuno and Palm Beach, Nate had deposited three of the men and all the supplies, including those for building the treehouse. With some time left before sunset, he decided to swing around Terminal City to make a special announcement. "Come tomorrow to the Curaray!" he shouted over the loudspeaker. The Indians seemed to look puzzled, but Nate wasn't dismayed. It was, after all, only the first try.

Wednesday, January 4, Nate and Pete took off for Palm Beach early, wanting to check out what was going on in Terminal City first. After observing little activity—Nate hoped that meant the Indians were on their way to the Curaray—the yellow plane landed on the soft sand of Palm Beach. Nate was pleased to see the treehouse built. After fixing the radio transmitter and checking in with Marj, he enjoyed a swim in the river. The others, meanwhile, took turns walking the beach, shouting Auca phrases into the forest, holding gifts in their hands. That evening, Nate and Pete returned to Arajuno for the night. The others had given them lists of supplies to bring back the next day.

On Thursday, after landing and unpacking, Nate and Pete walked along the beach and inland a bit, searching for tracks. There were numerous animal tracks, but also some human footprints, too. As Nate wrote in his diary, which he still was keeping at Palm Beach, among the wildlife were also "forty-seven billion flying insects." He and Pete ended the day by circling over Terminal City, again shouting the familiar invitation. They saw only one man, kneeling on a platform by one of the houses. He was facing the campsite and pointing with his hands.

That evening Nate wrote in his diary, "We find we have a friendlier feeling for these fellows all the time. We must not let that lead us to carelessness. It is no small thing to try to bridge between twentieth century and the stone age. God help us to take care."[1]

At around eleven in the morning on Friday, January 6, the

five missionaries were all on the beach. Roger, Ed, and Jim were on "beach patrol," walking and calling out Auca phrases as they had done many times before. Nate and Pete were sitting in the cooking shelter.

Suddenly, a voice from the forest answered Ed's call—a great, booming voice, speaking words that were unknown to the men. An Auca man then emerged from the forest, accompanied by two women, one in her thirties and the other around sixteen. They were, typically, unclothed, with strings tied about their wrists, waist, and thighs. The women wore large wooden circles in their ears.

Ed, trying to recover from his immediate shock, then responded with "Puinani," the Auca word for "welcome."

After a while, with help from Jim, the three Aucas approached the camp. Nate immediately began passing out gifts of paring knives and machetes, which they were enthusiastic to receive. He began taking pictures as fast as he could. They had to document their first actual meeting with this tribe.

Later that day, Nate took the man for a ride in the plane, circling slowly over the Auca village, to the great surprise of villagers who happened to glimpse one of their own somehow soaring above them. While the missionaries had invited their Auca guests to spend the night in the cooking shelter on the beach, only the older woman stayed, leaving shortly before the men arose the next day.

After that experience, Saturday was something of a letdown. No Aucas came to the campsite, despite more calls along the beach. When Nate circled over Terminal City in the afternoon, the sight of the plane sent what villagers were outside scurrying for shelter. He did manage to see the man who had come to Palm Beach on Friday, but even he looked less than pleased. He pointed to the plane and then seemed to smile at Nate, which reassured the pilot somewhat.

Sunday, January 8, Nate and Pete arrived at Palm Beach with a sense that this would be the day when more contact would be made. After breakfast on the beach, it was agreed that Nate would circle back over the Auca village to see if there was any activity. This time, he saw only women and children there. To Nate, that meant there was a good possibility that the men were on their way to the Curaray. Sure enough, on his return flight to the beach, he looked down and spotted at least ten men, walking in the right direction.

"This is it, guys!" Nate shouted upon landing. "They're on their way!" Nate radioed the same message at twelve-thirty to Marj, who was waiting at home for any news from her husband. They agreed he would check in again with her at four-thirty that afternoon.

At four-thirty, though, the radio was silent at Shell Mera.

By early Sunday evening the wives had been in touch with each other by radio, relaying the message that Palm Beach was silent. There was nothing they could do but wait. At daybreak the next day, chomping at the bit, Johnny Keenan was flying over the Curaray. Johnny didn't see any bodies, but he had ominous news to report. The frame of Nate's plane was sitting on the beach, ravaged of all its fabric. Together the wives agreed: It was time to involve the United States and Ecuadorean authorities, who immediately sent military personnel to the area as a search party.

While the wives waited at Shell Mera, the bad news came in spurts. By Wednesday, two bodies had been found. On Thursday, Ed's wristwatch was recovered by an Indian from Arajuno, but no body was discovered. Later that day, the military informed the wives that four bodies altogether had been recovered, but one, Ed McCully's, was probably lost forever down the river. The men had been speared to death.

Even though Nate and the four other missionaries were dead, Operation Auca was far from extinguished. MAF pilots continued making aerial drops into Auca territory, while Rachel Saint, who had been serving as a missionary elsewhere in Ecuador, began intensive language study with Dayuma. In late 1957, Betty Elliot and her daughter were stationed in Arajuno when two Auca women appeared in the jungle, seeking to make contact with Dayuma. Betty convinced them to come with her to Shandia, where Rachel was working with Dayuma. After a happy reunion, the Auca women, including Dayuma, returned to their village.

Weeks later, Marj Saint was visiting Betty and Rachel when they heard sounds of singing coming from the forest. There was Dayuma and the two other women, and seven other Aucas, singing "Jesus Loves Me."

Years later, in June 1965, when the name Auca was no longer used and the tribe's own name for themselves, Waorani, had been adopted, a baptism took place on the Curaray River. Just off the beach where Nate's yellow plane had been grounded, Kathy and Stephen Saint were baptized, along with two young Waoranis. Two tribal elders, Kimo and Dyumi, performed the ceremony. Nine years earlier Kimo and Dyumi had come to Palm Beach with spears poised. But where they had once killed, they now praised God for the gift of His Son.